THE JOINT FREE PUBLIC LIBRARY
of
Morristown and Morris Township
1 Miller Road, Morristown, N. J. 07960

MARIAN R. GERHART, *Director*

Tel. 538-6161
538-6162

November 8, 1982

Mr. James V. Costanzo
45 Crescent Drive
Convent Station, New Jersey 07961

Dear Mr. Costanzo,

What a warm and wonderful gift you have given to the Morristown Community. I have just read your book, New Neighbors, Old Friends, from cover to cover and shared laughter and tears, victory and setback, with the people in your story. You have indeed reached into the hearts of your subjects and told a story that is at once personal and universal.

We are so happy to add this long awaited book to our Local History Collection. Thank you for your generosity in sharing this material with others.

Sincerely,

Jeanne T. Will

Jeanne T. Will (Mrs.)
Local History Department

New Neighbors, Old Friends

Morristown's Italian Community
1880-1980

To Dr. Ronald J Grele,
Thanks in helping me in
the Oral history for this book.
Sincerely,
Jim Costanzo

by James V. Costanzo, Sr.

with an Introduction by
Dr. Francesco Cordasco
of Montclair (N.J.) State College

New Neighbors, Old Friends

Morristown's Italian Community
1880-1980

Collected from Family Albums
by James V. Costanzo, Sr.

with an Introduction by
Dr. Francesco Cordasco
of Montclair (N.J.) State College

Published by
The Morris County Historical Society
Morristown, New Jersey

Author: **James V. Costanzo, Sr.**
Project Coordinator/Senior Editor: **Dorianne Rose Perrucci**
Photography Editor/Art Director: **James V. Costanzo, Jr.**
Writer/Researcher: **Virginia Potter**

68 Morris Avenue, P.O. Box 170M, Morristown, New Jersey, 07960.

Published 1982.
Printed in the United States of America.

First Edition.

Includes index of photographs.

ISBN 0-910301-00-X
0-910301-01-A

Table of Contents

Dedication

This book of pictures and personal recollections is dedicated to my wife, Connie, and to our children, Jim, Jeanne and Marie, as well as to the parents, children and grandchildren of all Americans of Italian descent who grew up or lived in Morristown. I hope they will look with pride at these pictures and share the joy I have had in knowing most of Morristown's first Italians for over 60 years.

Moreover, I hope that all children of Italian descent will see reflected in these pictures a representation of their own parents and grandparents.

Our children must know that although their parents and grandparents came to this country practically penniless and unable to speak English, they brought with them great pride in their Italian heritage and a profound love for their families. Despite the sufferings, prejudices and humiliations they were subject to in the early years, our ancestors knew, deep in their hearts, that America was their only hope for opportunities to better themselves and their children. And they had the wisdom to know they had to earn it.

What hurt me in the twenties when I was a kid growing up and going to school was the attitude some people in town had towards the Italians living in The Hollow, particularly those on Flagler Street, without knowing anything about their dignity, pride or character. I often say that these people had everything the Vanderbilts, Astors and Whitneys had—except money.

That they eventually gained over time. In learning to speak English, though, I hope we remember to teach our children the language of the heart that distinguishes our people.

James V. Costanzo, Sr.

Acknowledgments

When I was a young man going through high school and then on to college, I fantasized about what it would be like to dress up our hardworking parents and grandparents and send them off to some fancy affair, like the exclusive "Four Hundred" event held each year at a grand hotel in New York City. If we exchanged their overalls and aprons for tuxedos and fancy ballgowns, could they be told apart from the others? I didn't think so.

That dream, childish as it may be, never did come true, but another has: the dream of presenting an enduring record of these people, the "unsung heroes" of history with their hopes and dreams. Thanks to The Morris County Historical Society, that dream has now become a reality.

I want to commend Robert Geelan, the Society's past president under whom this project began and Dr. Robert J. Fredericks, his successor, who saw this project through to completion, for their leadership; the Board of Trustees, that committed considerable funds to the project; and all Society members who, in publishing this book, recognize the achievements, not only of Morristown's first Italians, but of all immigrants.

Special thanks is due to Richard T. Irwin, Chairman of the Publications Committee, whose vision and energy sustained all of us from start to finish.

I am particularly grateful to the creative team that made my dream come alive: my son, James V. Costanzo, Jr., who served as Photography Editor and Art Director; Dorianne Perrucci, Project Coordinator and Senior Editor, whose persistence for perfection drove us beyond what we thought achievable on a short schedule; and Ginny Potter, Writer and Researcher, who worked with me since April, 1979, in transcribing my notes and interviews and indexing the pictures. A less dedicated trio would have given up several times over.

The willingness of several Morristown area residents to provide specific information gave this book its credibility as an historical record. They are: Marian R. Gerhart, Director of the Joint Free Public Library of Morristown and Morris Township; Mrs. Helen Pierson Hettinger of New York City, the daughter of The Neighborhood House's first directors; Mrs. Homer L. Meade, Executive Director of The Neighborhood House; Jack Schloerb, Director of the Morristown YMCA; and Mrs. Clifford Starrett, Chairwoman of the Building Committee at St. Peter's Episcopal Church in Morristown.

Pat Van Horn deserves special thanks for the exacting work demanded in indexing the pictures, and Nancy Salvini for contributing to the book's design.

The enthusiasm of several people who recognized the broader value of these pictures beyond their local significance was particularly encouraging to me. They are: Ronald J. Grele and Howard Green of the New Jersey Oral History Commission; and the late Dr. Clifford Lord, Director of the New Jersey Historical Society, whose attention was drawn to my collection by Fred Schmitt, a former researcher for the Society. Dr. Lord's interest in displaying pictures from my collection at the Society's statewide exhibit on ethnic history in April, 1979, inspired this project.

Also helpful was the publicity the initial display received from Ace Alagna, publisher of *The Italian Tribune*; Joan Babbage of *The Newark Star-Ledger*; and Margaret Farley, a longtime friend of the family formerly with the *Daily Record* in Morristown, New Jersey, who assigned Ginny Potter to cover the story.

Above all, I thank my friends and acquaintances from Flagler Street and the old neighborhood. Without them this book would not have been possible. They honored by persistence by painstakingly recalling details and reconstructing incidents that happened years ago, and they trusted me enough to let me borrow precious photographs to reproduce an affectionate and accurate record.

As a subjective history of Morristown's first Italians, please remember that the stories and events recorded here were recalled through the memories of those who lived them. Although every effort was made to check the accuracy of a fact and interpretation along with names and dates, some errors may remain. We cannot assume responsibility for them.

To all those, named and unnamed, who assisted me in this book, I remain, with deepest appreciation and gratitude,

Sincerely,

James V. Costanzo

July, 1982

Topics of the Times

A Surprise for the Uplifters

March 14, 1914

That usually submissive worm, "the poor," has turned, for once, and made a vehement, even violent, protest against playing its long familiar role as subject for investigation, exhibition, exclamation, exhortation, and reformation by its self-confident betters in the upper circles. This phenomenon, the surprising quality of which, for some of us, is its unfamiliarity, is reported from New Jersey, long famous as the land of strange people and happenings, and the town which it puts on the map is Morristown.

Some of the "best people," there, acting with characteristic excellence of intention—and on the not less characteristic assumption that they alone dislike to have their private affairs, misfortunes, follies, and vices disclosed to the public—have recently made, or procured the making of, a "social survey." As might have been expected, the observations of the surveyors, if not entirely limited to, were only productive in, the least prosperous quarters of the town, which chanced to be the Italian colony, and it was discovered that not a few of the colonists were living in the conditions which penury and ignorance commonly combine to produce.

The next step was to arrange a "social survey exhibit" of photographs and charts, showing just what those conditions were. Such an exhibit is doubtless interesting, and it might serve much better ends than the satisfying of curiousity, either sympathetic or morbid. Unfortunately, some of the people photographed and charted visited the show, and they very strongly objected to the employment of themselves, their children, and their homes as "horrible examples." They did more—they proceeded to destroy the exhibits, then and there, and to threaten more desperate roughness if what they chose to think was a holding of themselves up to scorn did not cease.

One cannot commend this form of rebellion against "uplifters," but it is not incomprehensible, and the episode might well serve as a lesson for people who, with the very best of motives, act as if "feelings" ceased to exist below the level of "comfortable circumstances." Perhaps they used to do so, but times are changing.

Documenting History:
A Perspective on the Self-Portrait
by James V. Costanzo, Jr.

The *New York Times* article of March 14, 1914 ("A Surprise for the Uplifters") raises some interesting questions concerning the nature of the photographic image.

The life of Italian immigrants in Morristown, New Jersey, at the turn of the century was not substantially different from the plight of other minority ethnic groups newly arrived in this country: long, hard work for low pay; segregation in an ethnic "colony"; discrimination and verbal slurs directed towards their racial and national origins.

Why, then, did these people, who seemed to passively accept poverty and discrimination as part of their daily lives, react so violently; not against their immediate living conditions, but against the representation of their lives presented in that exhibit?

The answer lies in the intrinsic nature of the photograph, which cannot be understood apart from its social, cultural and historical contexts. The camera may be only a mechanical tool, but it is directed and activated by the human will which governs the shape of one's self-image.

Unfortunately, photographs from the original exhibit could not be located. If they were available, doubtless they would confirm what the newspaper article points to: The Italians documented themselves differently than the "uplifters" did. The immigrants took photographs of themselves and of each other that vigorously showed they did not see themselves as helpless victims of the immigration system.

In contrast, the work of most documentary photographers was concerned with publicizing the poverty and degradation of the helpless in order to provoke social change.

Jacob Riis, a journalist, began photographing the slums of New York, particularly the poor living conditions of Italian immigrants, at the turn of the century. When published, his photographs caused a scandal that helped to establish a form of public housing.

Lewis Hine began photographing immigrants, Italians and others. Later he focused on other subjects of social concern. Hine is best known for his photographs exposing the poor working conditions of children; in fact, his photographs are credited as a major factor in the passage of child labor laws.

As the work of these two photographers demonstrated, documentary photography can be a powerful and positive tool in influencing and changing how society views itself and its responsibilities.

The photographs in this book, however, are distinctly different from most documentary work. As important as their work might be, professional photographers are not really involved with their subjects. They are outsiders looking in, and this shows in the resulting images they record. In representing immigrants, for instance, Riis and Hine showed the world typical "immigrants" suffering in the midst of impoverished circumstances, not individuals with names and faces who believed they had distinct destinies.

On the contrary, most of the images in this book came directly from the individuals "documented"; in fact, they made the initial selection of photographs. This is important in accounting for the personal and intimate ambience that distinguishes the collection. These are not stereotyped images taken by strangers of other strangers; they are photographs of Italians taken by other Italians, the type of images kept as a fond remembrance of a loved one, collected and cherished as part of family history and legend.

This book, however, is more than just the personal "album" of a particular community of people. It is an historical record.

Before the statewide exhibit sponsored in April, 1979, by The New Jersey Historical Society, the late Dr. Clifford J. Lord, then its Director, wrote to my father. "The photographic collection you have put together on the Italians in the Morristown area is a unique archive . . . I know of no comparable photographic record extending over so many years of any group, ethnic or otherwise, in any other community in the nation . . ."

In looking through this book, many people, Italian or not, will comment that a particular photograph reminds them of themselves or someone they know. That really doesn't come as a surprise. After all, we are all part of the extended human family; and history—if the larger picture of reality is considered—is an extended personal record.

(James V. Costanzo, Jr., who served as Photography Editor, received a Master of Fine Arts degree from the University of Iowa. He is the son of the author.)

From Old World to New: The Changing Italian Experience

by Dr. Francesco Cordasco

To much of American society, the Italian experience in America begins—and ends—with the notorious stereotypes presented in the movie version of *The Godfather.*

To the contrary, the Italian experience defies and defeats these stereotypes if it is accurately understood in relation to its three historical periods:

The large-scale emigrations from Italy beginning in the 1880's and ending in the mid-1920's, when immigration restriction and quotas terminated the massive Italian entry into the United States; the second period of generational conflict and acculturation, extending from the excluding legislation of the 1920's to World War II and the mid-1950's; and the third period, still evolving, dominated by the children and grandchildren of American-born Italians now into the third and fourth generations. The Italians in each of these periods are so much different in their experiences, needs and interrelationships with the larger American society that they may conveniently be labeled *Italian Italians, Italian Americans,* and *American Italians.*

In 1524, Giovanni da Verrazzano, commanding a French vessel, sailed up New York Bay, a little less than 100 years before Henry Hudson sailed up the Hudson River in 1609. Prior to and after the American Revolution, Italian cultural influence in New York City manifested itself in the ever-growing number of Italian musicians such as Nicholas Biferi, the Neapolitan harpsichordist, and Lorenzo Da Ponte, who contributed to the growth of the opera.

New York also became a haven for political refugees, the most famous of whom was Giuseppe Garibaldi, who led the unification of Italy. Other distinguished Italians who arrived in New York City before the Civil War included: G.P. Morosini, a partner to Jay Gould; Louis Tinelli, a pioneer in silk manufacturing; Giuseppe Tagliabue, an inventor and manufacturer of hydrographic and meteorological instruments; and Luigi Palma di Cesnola, U.S. Consul in Cyprus and the first director of the Metropolitan Museum of Art.

Until 1870, however, Italian immigration to the United States was an individual and sporadic phenomenon. After 1885, it became a mass migration of family groups and village units from South Italy which continued without interruption until the outbreak of World War I in 1914. The magic name of America was escape from the hopeless and intolerable living conditions of the *contadino* (peasant) and, to a great extent, the *artigiano* (artisans and small merchants) class as well.

Only with the beginning of mass emigration did the Southern Italian peasant show any outward and active desire for change. According to the historian Pasquale Villari, emigration was a form of revolt which saved Italy from fierce and bloody uprisings among the Southern Italian peasants.

Italians in the Old World: The Revolt Against Serfdom

The *Risorgimento* led by Garibaldi had proclaimed freedom of the individual, but it remained, as far as the *contadino* was concerned, only a proclamation.

The *contadino* continued to exist in a state of subservience to the landowner. Under the strictly enforced caste system, he was excluded from participation in local affairs and received no encouragement toward giving up his traditional attitude of passive disinterestedness.

Social conditioning, due to centuries of living according to accepted tradition, clan affiliations and a lack of group leadership, had ill prepared the *contadino* for a successful struggle on behalf of individual or class rights. The *contadino* functioned only as a member of his individual family unit and the larger unit, the *famiglia* (clan).

The village was the social unit, and the family was the basic unit of Southern Italian society. Economically, socially and culturally, the village was an almost self-sufficient entity. The mountain chains in Southern Italy contributed to this isolation; the only large cities were Naples, Palermo, Catania and Messina. Local dialects and regional restrictions on intermarriage were further divisive factors.

The all-powerful embrace of the *famiglia* circumscribed the daily activities as well as the social horizon of the Italian *contadino.* The family in Southern Italy was an extended social group that included all blood relatives and in-laws up to the fourth degree. To the Southern Italian, the family was an all-inclusive social world, and in a *contadino* community, the population consisted of a number of familial groups. The basic code of the *famiglia* was family solidarity and the exclusion of outsiders. Family leadership, vested in one male member of the larger family whose authority was unquestioned, was the mainstay of this familial organization.

From the isolated villages and towns of Southern Italy, the mass migration got under way in increasing momentum until, in the record year of 1907, about 300,000 Italians arrived at Ellis Island in New York City. At this port of entry, within a few decades, there was enacted a social drama involving the greatest concentration of Italians anywhere in the world—more Italians, in fact, than in the cities of Rome or Naples or Milan.

Although it has been fashionable for Italians, like other American ethnic groups, to "discover" themselves involved in the earliest European incursions into the New World (After all, didn't Columbus discover America?) and to see themselves as participants in the formation of the United States, the Italian presence in this country was not significant until the late 19th century. The Census of 1850, the first to distinguish between nationalities, recorded only 3,645 Italians in the United States; 44,230 were counted in the 1880 Census.

Beginning in 1880, however, until the immigration quotas imposed in the mid-1920's, Italian immigrants to the United States swelled to a floodtide; 300,000 entered this country from 1881-1890; 600,000 from 1891-1900; and two million from 1901-1910. The Italian immigrants of this early period, as well as those who continued to pour into the United States until the gates were closed in the mid-1920's, were *Italian Italians* in America whose experiences were significantly different from those of their offspring born in the New World.

Italians in the New World: The Price of Freedom

In establishing himself in the New World, the Italian immigrant followed the pattern common to all immigrants. Out of compulsion, because he was rejected by the older established groups, as well as inclination because of the social law of "consciousness of kind," he sought refuge and security in those areas of the city which earlier immigrant groups abandoned as undesirable. Italians did not create the slums; they simply took them over from other immigrant groups.

The earliest Italian "colonies" or communities were in lower Manhattan in New York City. The Northern Italians, mostly Genoese, established themselves around Washington Square in Greenwich Village and around 59th Street and Ninth Avenue. The Southern Italians were herded into the squalor of Mulberry Street and the notorious Mulberry Bend, the oldest of the "Little Italys." A second Italian community was established in East Harlem, which at its height in the 1930's had a population of 90,000.

Subsequently and almost simultaneously, Italian-American communities were created mainly by Sicilians and Calabrians around Arthur and Haight Streets in the Bronx. All the Southern Italian provinces (Campanie, Le Puglie, Lucania, Calabria, Sicilia, Abruzzi) colonized an area in South Brooklyn, around President, Hackett, Columbia and Bergen Streets, as well as other areas in Williamsburg, East New York and Long Island City. The colony in Ozone Park was unique because it was settled by Italian Americans from all the Italian provinces, both North and South.

These parent communities not only maintained themselves, but as Italian immigration increased in momentum, the earlier arrivals, dissatisified with living conditions in the district of their first settlement, followed the trend towards the outside of the expanding metropolis and founded other colonies. In a study based on the Census of 1930, there were 39 areas in Greater New York where from 30 to 90 percent of the population was Italian in origin.

Practically all Italian-American groupings and social organizations, geographical and cultural, were on the basis of the *paese* (town or village) of their origin. Group thinking, feeling and action centered so exclusively about the *paese* and *paesani* (fellow villagers and townsmen) that in Italy, a very apt expression, *campanilismo* (village mindedness), had been coined.

Although the immigrant did not take with him the institutions of his native village, he did take two important social concepts which had an important bearing upon his development in his new milieu: *campanilismo* and *la famiglia.* He lived by this code to the point where, in the new environment, it was not at all exceptional to find whole families and *paesani* occupying the tenement houses of a New York City block, doing business with or having their social life strictly within this group and being suspicious and antagonistic even to compatriots who came from other towns of the same province.

In the intervening years, under the impact of the American environment with its emphasis on the individual and its extreme mobility, regional differences were blurred, keen local prejudices were blunted and marriage barriers were broken down. Until 1940, however, the basic unit of the social organization was still the *paesano,* the mutual aid society and particularly family cohesion and solidarity. An important aspect of the acculturation process of the Italian has been the power of his traditional family culture to survive in strength in the American milieu even among the third generation through the 1970's.

When the Italian immigrant came to the United States, he had little or no experience with institutional life. He was hardly aware of the existence of the school as an institution, and, although Roman Catholic by tradition, he was merely a passive participant in the various services conducted in the village church by the clergy. The towns and villages back in Italy had neither a local press nor a local bank. Moreover, he was a disinterested, unconcerned spectator in the limited political life of the town or village.

Consequently, when he settled in the New World, he found himself at a tremendous disadvantage. A highly organization-minded society confronted him, with extremely well-developed impersonal secondary group relations oriented away from the primary group face-to-face relations of the closely knit *famiglia* and the all-inclusive *paese*.

Not surprisingly, he gave his immediate attention to those institutional forms with which he was most familiar: the family, the church and the mutual aid society.

The Italian immigrant tried to establish a replica of the *famiglia* pattern by bringing to America as many of the family unit as possible, attempting to find lodging in the same tenement and on the same block, and seeking work that would keep them together. In a study in East Harlem's Little Italy, it was found that many of the elements of the family mores continued as a potent influence among *Italian Americans* of the second and third generation; elements obscured by outward and superficial aspects of "Americanization" but still operative. The geographic segregation of the Italian immigrant strengthened this cultural pattern and gave it a long lease on life.

The establishment of exclusively Italian-American Roman Catholic churches was a more difficult task for the new immigrants. The language, culture and religious traditions, particularly the characteristic religious street festivals of the Southern Italian immigrant, were alien and objectionable to other Roman Catholics, but they made possible a distinctly Italian Catholic Church.

Eventually Roman Catholic churches in Italian-American communities were either taken over by Italians or built by the joint efforts of the faithful in the Italian-American community and the various Roman Catholic religious orders recruited from Italy, such as the Jesuits, Dominicans, Franciscans and Salesians. By 1940, there were some 80 churches in the Archdiocese of New York and Brooklyn which were dominated by Italian parishioners and many Italian priests, most of them trained in Italy.

To the purely religious function of the church were added parochial schools, recreational facilities and semi-religious societies which sponsored many secular programs. There were also picturesque religious processions and rituals characteristic of Southern Italy which had survived in their pristine strength. These festivals were social events of great significance eagerly anticipated by the Italian community every year. Hardly a week passed from early summer to fall without a *festa* being held to honor a local patron saint of one of the towns or cities in Sicily, Calabria, Le Puglie, Basilicata or Campania. The most outstanding yearly festival, which took place in East Harlem on July 16, was the Festival of Our Lady of Mt. Carmel.

Like the *famiglia* and the church, the mutual aid society was an important component of the Italian-American community. Dedicated to mutual aid and protection in case of sickness, death or other misfortune, its membership was recruited exclusively from the *paese*. It not only constituted the heart of the *contadino's* social life in America, but it was their continuing point of contact with the town or *paese* from which they came.

The federation of many of these and other societies into the Order of Sons of Italy in America was a natural sequence, and in New York City and New York State, under the leadership of Supreme Court Justice Salvatore Cotillo, Mayor Fiorello La Guardia, and Judge Ferdinand Pecora, the Order became politically conscious. The advent of Fascism caused a split in the Order, and the Sons of Italy, Grand Lodge, New York State with 50,000 members seceded because of a disagreement of the parent body with political Italy. Attempts to create lodges of second-generation Italians have not proven too successful. The mutual aid society was created by the first generation immigrants, and it largely died off when these hardy pioneers passed on.

The New Italian-American Consciousness

Italian-American studies are growing; the proliferation of monographs, books and scholarly articles (often emerging out of doctoral theses) attests to this vitality.

Considering that the Italian-American community numbers at least 21 million in the United States, this *Risorgimento* in Italian-American studies was long overdue. Two questions need to be asked: Why has scrutiny of the Italian-American community been so intense in recent years? And why has the study of a group long resident in the United States come so late?

The answer to the first question is clear. The new ethnic interest was sparked by the Civil Rights Movement of the last two decades and the black consciousness which accompanied it. The new ethnicity among Italian Americans to understand themselves was catalyzed by the search for "roots" which gripped all Americans in the 60's. The founding of the Italian-American Historical Association in that same decade is understood in this context.

Why Italian-American studies developed so late is a much more complex question to answer. As we noted earlier, the majority of Italians who migrated to the United States during the period of the great migrations (1880-1920) were Southern Italian *contadini*. They were wretchedly poor and easy targets for manipulative oppression, discrimination and cultural assault.

Their late arrival in America made success and achievement elusive and more difficult for them than it had been for earlier people like the Irish or the Germans. Their American-born children, caught up in a storm of complex changes, were scrutinized by a battery of psychologists, social workers, educators and sociologists. As the first large and seemingly intractable mass which threatened the established mores and economy of American society in a relatively short period of time (four-fifths of the Italian immigrants entering the United States came during the years 1901-1914), it is not difficult to understand why they were treated like a minority group.

Besides that, Italians were the victims of their own village-mindedness or provincialism *(campanilismo)* which they transplanted from the villages of South Italy to the teeming urban ghettos in the cities of America. Mystically medieval Catholics, Italians were also inhospitably rejected for the most part by the American Irish-Catholic church.

Certainly such a past was not to be envied or nostalgically pursued. This oppressive burden of the past has been further exacerbated by the stigma of crime. As Alexander De Conde has noted: "In the popular mind, the connecting of Italians with crime was as American as associating Jews with shady business deals, Irishmen with boss politics or Negroes with watermelons."

Italian Americans thus began studying their own past only after they had become established and secure socially and financially, and after enough intellectuals had been educated in the second and third generations. The responses of Italian immigrants to American society, like the contexts in which they occurred, have not been easily defined or understood.

It remains an unresolved question today whether Italian Americans have yet divested themselves of the pejorative connotations of this past treatment.

There is a great deal of literature which deals with Italian-American and American society. This literature, essentially an investigation of intergroup relations, is all interrelated to some degree. Usually these investigations begin with studying group relations among Italians themselves, as well as an application of what is understood as "interethnic" relations (e.g., Italians and the Irish; Italians and the Jews). The intricacies of American politics are also explored from this point of view, with elaborate explanations for the failures or, at best, modest successes by Italian Americans in this field.

Inevitably, however, the greater themes of acculturation and assimilation are introduced, which point out how Italian Americans have adapted to American culture. This greater framework presents difficulties, not only because of the subtleties which exist in any study of acculturation, but particularly because of the peculiar identification with crime which always enters in any discussion of Italian Americans; the "curse of the Mafia," as Nathan Glazer and David P. Moynihan have phrased it.

Glazer and Moynihan do not have the answer, except to suggest that "there may have been some displacement of anti-black feeling to Italians [and that] society needs an unpopular group around, and the Italians were for many reasons available." (Glazer and Moynihan, 1970, pp. lxvi—lxviii).

At best it is difficult to deal retrospectively with the multifaceted responses of Italians to American society. It is also too early to assess the new ethnic consciousness manifested by Italian Americans in the present period. There is some truth in this observation:

"Clearly, many Italian Americans are today responding to the complicated forces loosed by their assimilation into the American mainstream. The children of Italian immigrants no longer feel Italian: They are American . . . In shedding a sense of apartness from American life, they have also relinquished their once-powerful emotional association with a remote Italian world that they knew secondhand, from family recollections and legends. A void has been created, and they are now beginning to reevaluate their ethnic past—which is Italian American rather than Italian—because it is an inescapable part of what they think about themselves, and what they tell their children." (Erik Amfitheatrof, 1973, p. 324)

Alexander De Conde gives the next generation of Italians in America this challenge:

"Although it is true that immigrant peoples in the second and third generation largely lose their language and culture, are transformed by the pressures for conformity in American society, are stripped of their original attributes, and are recreated as something new, some, such as Italian-Americans, are still identifiable as distinctive groups." (Alexander DeConde, 1971, p. 380)

It has not been said better. In reevaluating their ethnic past, Italian Americans will continue their unique experience in an evolving American society.

Bibliography

Amfitheatrof, Erik. *The Children of Columbus: An Informal History of the Italians in the New World.* Boston: Little, Brown, 1973.

Cordasco, Francesco. *Italians in the United States: A Bibliography of Reports, Texts, Critical Studies, and Related Materials.* New York: Oriole Editions, 1972.

Cordasco, Francesco. *The Italians: Social Backgrounds of an American Group.* New York: Augustus M. Kelley, 1974.

Cordasco, Francesco. *Italian Americans: A Guide to Informational Sources.* Detroit: Gale Research, 1978.

Cordasco, Francesco. *Italian Mass Emigration. The Exodus of a Latin People. A Bibliographical Guide to the Bollettino Dell' Emigrazione, 1902-1927.* Totowa, N.J.: Rowman and Littlefield, 1980.

Covello, Leonard. *The Social Background of the Italo-American School Child: A Study of the Southern Italian Family Mores and Their Effect on the School Situation in Italy and America.* Edited and with an Introduction by Francesco Cordasco. Leiden, The Netherlands: E.J. Briss, 1967.

Cubberley, Ellwood P. *Changing Conceptions of Education.* Boston: Houghton Mifflin, 1909.

DeConde, Alexander. *Half-Bitter, Half-Sweet: An Excursion into Italian American History.* New York: Scribner's, 1971.

Gambino, Richard. *Blood of my Blood: The Dilemma of the Italian Americans.* New York: Doubleday, 1974.

Images: A Pictorial History of Italian Americans. New York: Center for Migration Studies, 1981.

Iorizzo, Luciano J., and Salvadore Mondello. *The Italian-Americans.* Second Edition. Boston: Twayne, 1980.

Kramer, Judith R. *The American Minority Community.* New York: Crowell, 1970.

Lopreato, Joseph. *Italian Americans.* New York: Random House, 1970.

Professors' Religious and Ethnic Backgrounds: The 1975 Ladd-Lipset Survey of U.S. Faculty Members. *The Chronicle of Higher Education,* Sept. 22, 1975.

Rolle, Andrew. *The American Italians: Their History and Culture.* Belmont, Calif.: Wadsworth, 1972.

Rolle, Andrew. *The Italian Americans: Troubled Roots.* New York: The Free Press, 1980.

Francesco Cordasco, a sociologist and cultural historian teaching at Montclair State College, has taught at Long Island University, City University of New York, New York University and the University of Puerto Rico. He received his B.A. degree from Columbia University and his M.A. and Ph.D. from New York University.

The author of many books on Italian Americans, Dr. Cordasco has written extensively on ethnicity and ethnic communities in the United States, educational sociology, urban education and the immigrant child in American schools. He served as Advisory Editor for the 39-volume work, *The Italian American Experience* (Arno Press/New York Times, 1975).

Professor Cordasco also serves as a trustee of the Society for the Advancement of Education. In 1967 he received the Brotherhood Award of the National Conference of Christians and Jews, and in 1976 the Order of Merit by the Republic of Italy "for outstanding contributions to the Italian community in America."

"I had in mind a subjective history—what was in their hearts and minds; their innermost thoughts, secrets, ambitions, desires. To tell the story from inside the person—that is what we wanted to penetrate . . ."

James V. Costanzo, Sr.

In 1931, James Costanzo, Sr. (center) met his grandfather, Vincenzo Costanzo. **Benevento, Italy.**

Prologue: Looking Back

"In 1931 when I was in law school, I went to Benevento, Italy. I met my grandfather Vincenzo for the first time. I stayed with him for two weeks, meeting his friends and getting to know my cousins and aunts and uncles.

"On the day I was to leave Benevento to come back home, my grandfather hired a carriage to take me from the village back to Naples to board the ship to America. I said goodbye to my grandfather and was halfway down the hill in the carriage when I looked back.

"Then it hit me. I would never again see my grandfather whom I had grown to love. I was 21, at the beginning of my life, and he was 75. Something inside of me cried, 'Go back, go back,' and I made the driver turn back. I embraced my grandfather and cried in his arms for a long time until I said goodbye.

"On the way back on the boat I could barely open my eyes for two days, knowing that I would never see my grandfather again."

James V. Costanzo, Sr.

Luigi and Maria Giovanna Meola with their sons (l-r): Nicholas, Luke, Dorfe, Anthony and Joseph. **c. 1920.**

Ever since he was a small boy, he dreamed of visiting the village in Italy where his father had been born.

In 1931, when he was 21 years old, ***Jim Costanzo*** visited Benevento near Naples. He was astonished to see its main street for the first time: It was a long and hilly dirt road that looked like Flagler Street back home in Morristown, New Jersey.

He was born in Morristown, a quiet and genteel town, on March 17, 1910; not uptown on "Millionaires' Row," but in "The Hollow," in that part of town where the Italian immigrants lived, along with a few Jewish and black families.

From 1880 to 1924 (when restrictive immigration quotas were imposed), over five million Italians entered this country. Like many others who had left their hometowns, Erminia and Dominick Costanzo, Jim's parents, were part of Morristown's early Italian community. They had met and married in 1907 on Flagler Street, where they owned and operated a grocery store.

As soon as he could count change, Jim, the second of four children, worked at the store every day after school and on Saturdays. It was there that he grew to know and to love the first Italians and their children. It was there, some 60 years ago, that this book began to take shape.

"When the older women spoke together in Italian with my grandmother, I'd stop and listen to them. They fascinated me. Most couldn't read or write English, but they were smart and full of vitality. There was something about them, some incredible spirit they had. I couldn't forget them."

When Jim Costanzo left Flagler Street in the late 20's to study law at Fordham University in New York City, he became one of Morristown's first Italian Americans to earn a law degree. He came back after he was graduated and established a practice in Morris County, which he later served as surrogate.

In the 1940's, busy with a growing family and a law practice, he began to seek out the first Italians. They were eager to relive their memories, and they talked with him for hours in Italian about "the old days." He wrote down the stories they told him.

"I began to feel that my children's lives—and the lives of other children—would not be complete unless they knew about these people, about their sacrifices and their unshakable determination to better themselves.

"They were willing to sacrifice anything to get ahead. They had the will to struggle against incredible odds, but they enjoyed life, too. I wanted my children and others to share the joy I had in knowing them."

The first Italians also showed him pictures from their family albums. He marveled at these photographs, many taken before 1900, which ranged from informal snapshots of the families at home, at work and at play on Flagler Street, to formal studio portraits that captured their way

Josephine and Giovanni Primavera with their children (l-r): Louis, Madeline and Mary. **c. 1911.**

of life in the rituals of baptism, Holy Communion, weddings and funerals.

He became convinced that he was seeing the pieces of a unique historical record, a collective portrait of one community which, like thousands of others, was shaping America at the turn of the century. He borrowed or copied these pictures and made countless phone calls and trips to complete his collection, often visiting children and grandchildren.

In April, 1979, when the New Jersey Historical Society sponsored a pictorial display of ethnic history at its headquarters in Newark, a researcher heard about Jim Costanzo's collection. The exhibit featured many of his pictures and stimulated considerable interest about the history of Italian families in Morristown.

In the spring of 1982, the Morris County Historical Society decided to sponsor publication of a documentary book and Mr. Costanzo donated his entire collection of over 1,000 photographs and negatives to the Society as an historical record.

Over 300 photographs are reprinted in this book. Although they are not comprehensive or conclusive, they vividly portray the history of an immigrant community and "tell" that history from an intimate point of view.

Most documentary photographers are strangers looking at strangers. They see their subjects as impersonal objects to be recorded. In contrast, the photographs in this collection are pictures of loved ones. The faces of parents and children, aunts and uncles, cousins and grandparents, look out from these pages.

Perhaps our struggle for success today is not as simple as the immigrants' struggle for survival was yesterday. Despite the differences, Mr. Costanzo believes their struggle has a message for us: Because they believed in themselves, they had the will to strive for a better future.

In fact, the early struggles were "exciting because we had ambition, and we had spirit, the spirit to do anything," recalled Jim's mother, ***Erminia Costanzo,*** who came to America in 1895 when she was five years old. Added ***John Stirone*** of a later generation: "Striving for something is one of the greatest feelings a person can have."

Through striving and sacrifice, self-reliance and selfless spirit, these immigrants survived and took root in a new land. It was the same for all those who came—and for those who continue to come—to America seeking a better way of life for themselves and for their children's children.

This is where the story begins, as told through the memories of the early Italians and their children, most of whom lived in the heart of Morristown's Italian section, on Flagler Street.

Mrs. Erminia Costanzo in her backyard on Water Street. **1929.**

Flagler Street as seen from the top of the hill, off Nicholas Avenue. **c. 1950.**

The backside of Flagler Street on Nicholas Avenue.

Vincenzo and Louisa Russo. **c. 1905.**

Mrs. Maria (Nunzia) Meola with her son, Pasquale. **Benevento, Italy, 1917.**

Josephine and Angelo Crisante with their daughter, Viola. **1913.**

Daniel and Mary Josephine Petrozzo with their sons, Patrick and Vito. **1913.**

Cesare and Maria DeFilippis with their children: (standing) John, Letizia, Peter; (second row, seated) Angelina and Jeanette; (front row) Josephine, Lucy and James.

Mrs. John (Filomena) Antonaccio.

Lucy and Margaret Antonaccio as children. **1920's.**

(right) In 1909, Vincenzo Costanzo journeyed to Morristown, New Jersey, to visit his first grandchild born in America. He posed with Alesandria (born in 1908) and his brothers Angelo and Raffaele, who worked in nearby Whippany.

(below) In 1931, Jim Costanzo (top row, center) returned the visit to meet his grandfather.

In 1913, (above) Erminia and Dominick Costanzo posed with three of their children (l-r): Nicholas, Alesandria and James. Almost 40 years later, their children's children posed for the picture to the left.

Constantino Bontempo with his children: Elminina (standing) and (l-r) Emilio, Anthony and Dominick. **Flagler Street, 1904.**

I. Flagler Street: A Place of Opportunity

"We lived on the third floor of the Marinaro building on Nicholas Avenue, a three-room, cold water flat. We were three boys and a girl in our family.

"My sister had her bed, and my two brothers and I slept in the next bed in the same room. Many times my two brothers' feet would hit me in the face, because I slept at the other end of the bed, and my head was at their feet!

"My brothers and I would say to my sister—who was a little older than we were—'Hey, when are you going to get married so we can have your bed?' That was life in those days, about 1925."

Ralph Cangelosi

Morris Common Pleas.

Jan. Term, 1899.

In the matter of the Final Application of

Carlo Garaffa

to be admitted to become a Citizen of the United States of America.

ON PETITION, &c.

Filed Dec. 28 - 1898

STATE OF NEW JERSEY,
COUNTY OF MORRIS, ss. } Joseph Lusardi

a witness produced by Carlo Garaffa the applicant in the above stated matter, who, being duly sworn, according to law, on his oath doth declare and say that he is a citizen of the United States of America, that he resides at #53 Speedwell Ave. Morristown NJ

and is personally well acquainted with Carlo Garaffa

the petitioner now before the Court: that said petitioner resides at Itallion Shanty Morristown,

Morris County, New Jersey, and that said petitioner has resided for five years within the United States and one year at least immediately preceding the presentation of his said petition within the State of New Jersey, and that during that time the said petitioner has behaved as a man of good moral character, attached to the principles of the Constitution of the United States, and well disposed to the good order and happiness of the same.

Sworn and subscribed in open Court this 6th day of Feb. A. D. 1899. } Joseph Lusardi

Wm. B. Ireland
Judge.

STATE OF NEW JERSEY,
COUNTY OF MORRIS, ss. } Carlo Garaffa

the petitioner, now before the Court, being duly sworn, according to law, on his oath doth declare and say that he resides at Itallion Shanty Morristown

Morris County, New Jersey; that he will support the Constitution of the United States, and that he doth absolutely and entirely renounce and abjure all allegiance and fidelity to every foreign prince, potentate, state or sovereignty whatever, and particularly to Umberto King of Italy

of which King he was heretofore a subject.

Sworn and subscribed in open Court this 6th day of Feb A. D. 1899. } Carlo Garaffa

Wm. B. Ireland
Judge.

Scarce or expensive housing is not a new phenomenon; many immigrants began life in the "promised land" in so-called "Italian shanties" where they lived for years before they qualified as citizens.

"The Golden Boat," as the Grupelli Flats on Flagler Street was called. **c.1920.**

One of the liveliest streets in Morristown in the early part of the century was a long, hilly dirt road named Flagler Street.

It was a street of poor but proud people in a town known for its mansions and millionaires.

Flagler Street lay in the heart of "The Hollow," bounded by Race, River, Spring, Water Streets and Nicholas Avenue. Although it ran only 300 yards off of Speedwell Avenue, one of the busiest thoroughfares in town, few of the elegant and wealthy citizens living uptown knew Flagler Street existed. Its low standing was social and economic as well as physical: Hundreds of Italian immigrants were crowded together in that quarter-mile.

On Flagler Street—the only dirt road in Morristown—dirt turned to dust in the summer and to mud when the nearby Whippany River overflowed its banks.

At the turn of the century, wooden apartment buildings called "flats" by the Italians lined the street. Built around 1875 by the Shelley family, they were three and four stories high, with narrow balconies in front and back and outhouses in the backyard. In good weather clothes were spread out to dry on the railings. Later Eney Grupelli, a prominent Flagler Street contractor, bought one of these buildings. Most of the first Italians lived in his building, known as "The Golden Boat" because of its shape, size (246′) and color.

In 1903, Nicholas Marinaro built two brick buildings, one on Flagler Street and another on Nicholas Avenue. They were considered better places to live because they were built of brick and had two toilets in the hallway.

Flagler Street was all the world the immigrants needed: They bought their food at Bontempo's and Petrozzo's at the top of the hill and baked their bread at Verrilli's Bakery near the bottom of the hill, on Race Street.

For many years, Bontempo's rivaled The Neighborhood House as the community's center of activity. At the store, passports could be issued and letters from home read or written to loved ones back in Italy. For many years the store also had the only phone on the street.

"Whenever someone wanted to call a family, they called that store and a messenger raced down the street shouting, 'You've got a call from your cousin in Newark,'" recalled ***Jim Costanzo.*** "That always caused a lot of excitement."

Next door to Bontempo's was The Neighborhood House and next to that was Goduto's Butcher Shop. Flagler Street was lined with stores, including Mainiero's Candy Store, DiFalco's Barber Shop, Calderaldo's Grocery, the Barone-Santoro Butcher Store, and Petrozzo's and Bozzi's groceries. In the middle of the street, for many years, was the Gurevitz Clothing Store.

At the bottom of the hill were two scrap metal businesses, Monoco's Dance Hall and the Cauldwell

Cauldwell Playground under water. **1919.**

Playground. The railroad tracks ran by Shelley's Ice House, alongside the Whippany River and Lake Pocahontas.

Life on Flagler Street spilled from the crowded flats onto the street outside. Children played in the dirt road and hurtled down the steep hill on homemade scooters, while women dressed in long black skirts shouted to one another across backyards. The delicious aromas of Italian food cooking on countless stoves filled the air. Women dried tomatoes on wooden boards outside to make tomato paste, while their men played *scopa* (cards), vigorously slapping the table each time they scored a point in their favorite game.

The immigrants did not talk about what was happening uptown. They did not know which royal person was visiting which millionaire, or how many thousands of dollars had been spent on staging another garden party. It was not their problem that noisy motor cars startled horses. Few motor cars even bothered to drive up or down Flagler Street's steep hill.

Only one tree, a mulberry tree, graced the street, which was a sharp contrast to the stately, tree-lined avenues uptown. With its convenience to New York City and its air of colonial gentility dating back to the American Revolution, Morristown had attracted more than 60 wealthy new industrialists who lived here at the turn of the century. Their combined net worth was estimated at half a billion dollars, which put Morristown on the map as "The City of Millionaires." Morristown was proud of its traditions dating back to the Revolution when George Washington chose the town as the site of the Continental Army's winter headquarters in 1777 and again in 1779-80.

By the time Morristown's millionaires were stepping onto the leisurely 9:30 morning train to Manhattan known as "The Millionaires' Express," Flagler Street's laborers were already at work, bending over pick and shovel.

As their husbands went off to work at dawn, Italian women began their day's work, too. By early morning clotheslines were heavy with the day's wash.

At dusk, men returned home, weary from working for 10 hours or more. Out of respect, their wives and children did not sit down to dinner until the man of the family came home. After the dishes were washed and put away, mothers and daughters often did piecework at night.

Tony Galdi's memories are typical. His oldest sister, Susie, who worked in Goodman's Blouse Factory during the day, "brought work home and worked on it until late at night." Others assembled umbrellas, earning 25¢ for every 12 completed.

Men, however, relaxed in the evenings by working in their gardens or by joining friends for a glass of wine and a game of *bocci* (lawn bowling).

Family gardens "were a paradise for us," recalled ***John Chiappa***. In addition, "There was a lot of vacant land near

Graduation party at Angelina (center) and Gabriele Imparato's farm. **Morristown, 1923.**

Lake Pocahontas which the town of Morristown owned. They loaned it to the Italians, who built shacks there with lumber supplied by the town. Men planted vegetables and relaxed in those little shacks after their long workdays."

Learning to use what was at hand—especially if it was free—was how the immigrants survived.

Louis Goduto described one of his daily chores during cold weather. "When I was a youngster, I carried many a bag of coal on my shoulders from the Lackawanna Railroad. We would go down to the roundhouse on Water Street to pick up the loose pieces. They filled 25 boxcars with coal to the top, and when the engineer came to a sudden stop, a lot of coal slid off. We used to be there with bags every day after school. We started from Morristown station and walked up to Morris Plains, one side of the track going up, the other side coming down."

Old railroad ties were also available free of charge if you were willing to use a little sweat, he continued. "When the railroad would replace the old ties with new ones, some of the families used to get together and hire a truck to do down and get them. About 10 families from the area met at the Grupelli Flats, and we'd take the ties and cut them into firewood for the stoves in the apartments. Each family got about 10 pieces.

"This was usually on a Sunday afternoon when the men cut those big ties into sizes to fit in the coal stove for firewood. We would sing in Italian while sawing the wood. There were big tubs of beer and wine for us when we got dry."

Ice, which kept food cold in hot weather, could also be found free, added ***Joseph Andresano.*** "At Shelley's Ice House on Water Street where I worked as a young man, we'd clean off the platform and push any loose or leftover pieces of ice outside. The pieces would fall to the ground, and people from the neighborhood would come with baskets and pails, and pans on their heads, to pick them up and take home."

Although not considered necessary for survival, scooters and bicycles were essential to a young boy's life. The dump at the end of Race Street near Lake Pocahontas was a good place to look for spare parts.

"The way we got a bicycle," said Mr. Galdi, "was to go the dump and look for broken wheels, twisted handlebars, anything to make a bike. We also put a wagon together from stuff we found there. Cleanup Day was a good day to find parts."

Flagler Street's steep hill was ideal for "winter sports." "We made toboggans that we rode down the street, going about 30 miles an hour," related ***Luke Soranno***. "We built a big snowbank about halfway down, about a foot high. When we came down at that speed, the sled leapt up like it was on a ski jump."

Pat Ninni (born in 1919) recalled another favorite "sport." "It was nothing for me, ***Frank Di Ruggiero,*** and the other kids to walk on the porch railings at the back of

Anna Petillo and Vincent Pennimpede with their wedding party. **1927.**

our building on the third or fourth level. That was 40 or 50 feet up in the air because the land sloped in the backyard. We weren't scared because we didn't know any better. If our parents had seen us, they would've either fainted or killed us."

In the summertime, nearby Lake Pocahontas was used at various times of the day as a swimming hole by the youngsters, a "laundromat" by the women and an outdoor bath by the men.

"We had no bathroom or shower in our apartment, so my father and many of the older men went down to Lake Pocahontas to bathe," continued Mr. Ninni. "Pop left his underwear on, soaped himself up and went under the falls where they had put up long planks so the water fell like a shower."

In good weather everybody lived outside, Mr. Galdi added.

"When it was hot, all the old people sat outdoors, and the children played outdoors, too. Everybody got together to talk, talk, talk. During the holidays, especially Christmas and Easter, all the older women exchanged baked goods. 'I'll bring you something I made, and you give me something you baked,' they would say to each other. There was plenty to eat for everybody. Folks used to talk most of the night, and the kids played on the porches. The younger ones went to bed and the old people still stayed on the porches talking. It was pretty good in those days."

Music filled the air during balmy weather. On a summer night, music carried up the street from Monoco's Hall where the band held rehearsals twice a week, parading up and down while they practiced for civic gatherings. Most of its members were Italian.

Frank DiPrimo remembers going up and down Flagler Street with his friends and stopping to serenade people in front of each flat. "We would be called inside and have a drink or two and then go on down the hill, stopping at each flat. Eat and drink and sing and play and make everybody happy. It didn't matter that we didn't get paid.

"If we had too much to eat and drink, we'd have to have our friends push us up the hill so we could get back home!"

People sang on those evenings as the music took them back to Italy, back to the homeland they had left because it offered them no future.

They spoke in Italian—on Flagler Street, they always spoke in their native tongue—of their struggles in this land of opportunity. And they remembered, with smiles and sadness, what they had left behind . . .

Vincent DiFalco's parents. **Benevento, Italy.**

Michael and Raffaella Sarinelli with their sons (l-r): Frank, Carmen and Dominick. **1921.**

Agnesina and Nicholas D'Aloise with their daughters, Vita and Dina. **c. 1920.**

Morristown society at the golf club. **1920's.**

Life on Flagler Street. **c. 1935.**

Aerial view of Morristown's "Hollow" in the Italian section. **c. 1940's.**

Carmine Cortese, who emigrated from Magisano in Calabria, Italy, in 1894.

Mr. and Mrs. Joseph Camisa, Morristown's first-known Italian immigrants, who arrived in 1880.

Filippo Goduto with his family.

Mrs. Filippo (Carmella) Nodoro with her children (l-r): Rocco and Andrew (back row); Mary and Vincent (front row). **Salerno, Italy, 1909.**

Emilio Leccese. **1915.**

Maria and Michael Cherello. **1915.**

Pietro Correale (r) with his parents, Caroline and Luigi. **1910.**

Maria and Luigi Corea with their children: Peter (back); Mary and Pauline (center); Sophia, Theresa and Dominick (front). **1919.**

Buddies: John Giordano, John Elia, Michael Galdi and Carmine Galdieri at Cauldwell Playground. **1927.**

"We had a lot of good athletes down there (at Cauldwell Playground). I played every sport they had: baseball, handball, tennis, softball, horseshoes, everything."

John Giordano

Joseph Antonaccio at Cauldwell Playground. **1910.**

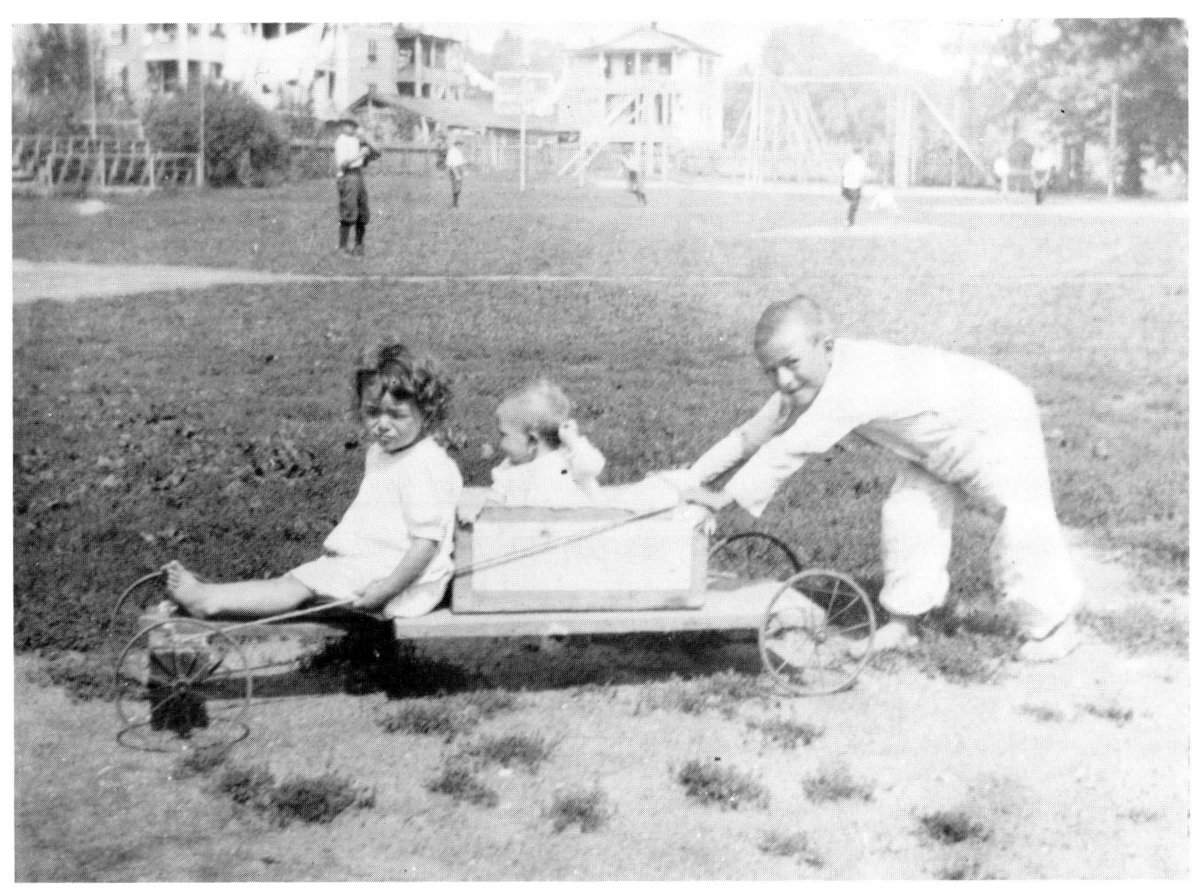

James Primavera pushing homemade wagon at Cauldwell Playground. **c. 1920.**

Flagler Street girls at Cauldwell Playground. **c. 1920.**

Party at Petrone's Farm. **1940.**

Celebrating at home: Angelo and Angelina Ninni (center) with their children and relatives.

Anniversary outing of The Montescaglioso Club and Band. **August, 1936.**

"We need more teachers for these bright children."

Mrs. Marie Pierson
Neighborhood House
Annual Report, 1916

Flagler Street's "second home": The Neighborhood House. **1922.**

Cousins Agnes Butera and Phyllis Azzara at 18 years old.

Mrs. Frank Natale and daughter Nancy. **1934.**

Salvatore De Chiaro with his children. **1930's.**

Pietro and Jennie Milelli. **c. 1925.**

John and Sophia Chiappa.

Carmen and Michelene Pagano on their 50th wedding anniversary.

Six little Nobiles. **1934.**

"Although it is true that immigrant peoples in the second and third generation largely lose their language and culture, are transformed by the pressures for conformity in American society, are stripped of their original attributes, and are recreated as something new, some, such as Italian-Americans, are still identifiable as distinctive groups."

Alexander DeConde

. . . and how they grew! Mrs. Nunziata Nobile (center) with daughters Donna and Mary (back row); Rose, Philip, Lucy and Joseph (front row).

All grown up: Mrs. Nobile at daughter Rose's wedding to Carmine DeBiase. **June 24, 1951.**

Fedele and Mary Lucia with their daughters. **1902.**

II. The Voyage Over: Shelter of the Extended Family

All Flagler Street knew Antonio's joy and anticipation that morning in September, 1903, when he boarded the train to meet his wife and young son, who had arrived at last in New York City. With growing impatience, he strode back and forth across the cavernous waiting room on Ellis Island, searching for the sign that indicated where passengers from the S.S. Calabria *had disembarked.*

He looked into hundreds of unfamiliar faces. When he could not find his wife and son in the crowd, he approached two customs officials for help. They took him to a ship's officer who seemed startled when Antonio told him his name.

Slowly, speaking softly in Italian, the officer told Antonio that his wife had died of fever on the voyage over.

So many women had died aboard the ship, the officer hastened to explain, and the fever had been so fierce and spread so quickly, that the captain had been forced to do away with burial ceremonies.

A few minutes later Antonio Sansone was introduced to his four-year-old son, Larry, whom he had kissed goodbye more than three-and-a-half years before in Foggia, Italy.

Larry's first words to the grieving, sobbing man who held him so tightly, were: "They threw my mother's body in the ocean."

Larry Sansone

Larry Sansone and Mary Mazzone with their wedding party. **1929.**

News of sorrow spread quickly on Flagler Street.

Antonio's friends rallied around him, giving him strength and support. They took his small son into their arms, seeking to comfort this child whose arrival in America had been so sad.

Antonio continued to board with Mrs. (Remigio) Antoinette Galdi and her family at 16 Flagler Street, and Larry lived with him in a room crowded with other boarders. Larry was the only child who boarded with the Galdis, but he was special. Mrs. Galdi took care of him during the day while his father worked.

At this point, it can be assumed that Antonio Sansone's story is typical. Undoubtedly, the Sansone family in Foggia, Italy, did what thousands of other peasant families all over Italy did at the turn of the century: They met to decide which member of the family should seek a new life in America. Antonio was chosen, and the money for his passage scraped together.

There was no question where he would settle. He would go to a town in America where others from Foggia had recently settled, a small town in northwest New Jersey not far from New York City.

Antonio knew he would find work in Morristown. *Paesani* would help him find a job with the railroads or on a nearby estate. The newspapers in Italy were full of advertisements from American companies looking for workers.

Work was plentiful in the new country, and there were other differences too. In Morristown, Italians from Salerno, Naples and Benevento by the Mediterranean Sea, on the west coast, mixed freely with villagers from Bari and Foggia on the east coast, near the Adriatic Sea, from Catanzaro in the province in Calabria and from Palermo on the island of Sicily.

As a rule, strangers were not accepted into a family on Flagler Street. There was a bond, usually tied to the village in Italy that was birthplace for both the transplanted family in America as well as the newly-arrived immigrant. Boarders quickly became part of the family and stayed for several years, usually up until they married and moved out.

Boarding with a family gave the newcomer a sense of belonging before he left Italy and extended Flagler Street's "family" as acquaintances from the village back home became old friends in America. The boarder, without a family of his own, had a place to call home where he did not have to worry about cooking and cleaning. And the Italian housewife doubled her influence by doubling the family income.

When a family decided to take in boarders, word was sent back to the village that space was available. Later, when a man decided to leave Italy, he could plan to go to Morristown even before he boarded ship. Weeks later when he knocked on the door of a flat to ask for a room,

Larry Sansone with his family. **1950's.**

he knew about the family inside—and they knew about him.

Foggia, a village on Italy's Adriatic Sea, had lost many young men like Antonio to America. They left because there was no hope for them in Italy, particularly South Italy, which was largely agricultural.

Italy's caste system was a prison left over from feudal times. If a man were born a peasant, he died a peasant. If he were born rich, he remained rich. The only "inheritance" a peasant could pass on to his children was a life of poverty. It had been that way for grandfathers; it would be that way for grandsons.

Italy's peasants were tenant farmers who were paid little or no wages for unending labor that filled their days from dawn to dusk. They existed on that small portion of the yearly harvest which they were allotted.

For hundreds of years, peasants had been locked into a grim and unrewarding way of life in a country often at war with itself. Despite unification under Giuseppe Garibaldi in 1861 and promises of equality, no new life reached down to the peasant.

Peasants continued to live without hope until late in the 19th century when stories about America began spreading: America, land of hope. America, land of opportunity.

They said a man could earn money there—and spend it as he wished. He could change his life through his own energies—and be free: free to buy land, free to better his life, free to better his family's life.

In America, they said, there was promise and opportunity, if a man was willing to work. But the only way to seize the promise was to leave Italy—forever.

Letters sent back home confirmed the story: In America it *was* different. Peasants who had earned only food and board were earning more than a dollar a day.

One morning in 1900, Antonio had embraced his wife, his infant son, his parents and many relatives and friends, and turned to leave behind him all that was fond and familiar.

Never again would he return to his village. His family accepted the loss because they believed a man must use his ambition where it counted, and America was a land of opportunity.

Aboard the ship that would take him to America, Antonio was assigned a dirty straw mattress to sleep on. For one month he shared space with several hundred other countrymen crowded together in the bottom of the ship.

There were no windows in the room, no air to relieve the smell of sickness, no toilet facilities and no lanterns at night. Men and women were separated; children with their mothers.

Seasickness struck almost everyone at one time or another, and the few lemons distributed by crew mem-

Repara and Angelo Pennucci with their children, Joseph, Anna and Anthony. **c. 1931.**

bers did nothing to relieve the almost constant nausea. Women especially caught high fevers. Several people died on each voyage over.

Antonio survived the trip across, managing to hold onto his health as well as his suitcase. Some people had lost all their belongings, even savings hidden in waistbelts, when they were robbed by fellow passengers. Antonio had watched as a man wept helplessly while several of his countrymen stole his belongings and threw his empty suitcase overboard.

On Ellis Island Antonio endured a physical examination and was interviewed in Italian about his ability to work. He was glad when he was told he was free to leave.

His joy was mixed with bewilderment as he stepped off the Ellis Island ferryboat and into the confusion of New York City. Recruiters, speaking in Italian, shouted at him, offering him jobs.

Antonio made his way through the crowd, for he knew where he was going. Finding a train, the right train, was difficult until he found a *paesano* who pointed out the ferry to Hoboken, New Jersey. He searched again until he found a train heading in the right direction.

Once aboard, he realized he had no way of knowing when the train would arrive in Morristown. He appealed to the conductor who seemed to understand him. After what seemed like a long time, the conductor tapped him on the shoulder and pointed out the window as the train slowed down.

"Morristown. This is Morristown," the conductor said.

PINTO

Mrs. Pietro Pinto's family. **In Italy.**

Mr. and Mrs. Pietro Pinto with their family. **In America, c. 1925.**

BIANCHINI/MAZZONI

Agostino and Carolina Bianchini in the backyard of their home. **1906.**

The Bianchinis' daughter, Anna Maria, the day she was married to Serafino Mazzoni. **1920.**

CIAMPAGLIA/EVANGELISTA

Adelaide Ciampaglia (l) with her parents, Mr. and Mrs. Alfonso Ciampaglia. **Italy, 1904.**

Christina and Pio Ciampaglia, Adelaide's brother, with their children (l-r): Alfonso, Mary, Harry and Evelyn. **1913.**

Mrs. Adelaide (Ciampaglia) Evangelista with her daughters (l-r): Delia, Concetta and Enes. **In Italy, 1923.**

BOCCHINO

Concetta and Joseph Bocchino with their 13 children.

Concetta DiFalco on her wedding day to Joseph Bocchino. **1910.**

Concetta DiFalco (seated, left) with her parents Nicoletta and Ottavio and family. **In Italy, c. 1910.**

DiFALCO

Vincent DiFalco's father, Ottavio. **In Italy.**

Mr. and Mrs. Vincent DiFalco with their children. **1920.**

Mr. and Mrs. Vincent DiFalco with their children.

Mr. and Mrs. Vincent DiFalco with their grandchildren.

COSTANZO/DeNUNZIO

Lucia and Nicolo DeNunzio with their children. **c. 1905.**

Mrs. DeNunzio with her children and brother-in-law Felice (r). **1955.**

Erminia DeNunzio and Dominick Costanzo on their wedding day. **1907.**

The Costanzo and DeNunzio families, with friends. **1932.**

Costanzo and DeNunzio children and grandchildren.

MOSSO/PETRONE

Frank Mosso's parents and family. **In Italy.**

Giovanella and Pasquale Petrone with their children (l-r): Theresa, Carmine and Anthony. **1903.**

Theresa Petrone and Frank Mosso on their wedding day. **1914.**

VIGILANTE

Rose DeNunzio and Anthony Vigilante with their wedding party. **1920.**

Mary DePalma and Carmine Petrone with their wedding party. **1928.**

Rose and Anthony Vigilante with their son, Carmine and daughter, Helen. **1925.**

VIGILANTE

Carmine and Carmella Vigilante. **1920.**

Carmine and Carmella Vigilante with their children.

The expanded family: Carmella Vigilante (top row, center) with her children, grandchildren and great-grandchildren. **1951.**

"An important aspect of the acculturation process of the Italian has been the power of his traditional family culture to survive in strength in the American milieu even among the third generation."

Dr. Francesco Cordasco

Angela Michele D'Angelo. **c. 1915.**

III. Building a Home: Women at Work

Mrs. Lucia Mainiero and Mrs. Angela Michelle D'Angelo were typical of the women of Flagler Street in those early years.

Mrs. Mainiero, called Zia Lucia la zoppa, (for "Aunt Lucy who limps"), is remembered for her sharp business sense.

In addition to caring for her family, she took in 23 boarders by renting the basement apartment below Bozzi's Grocery next to her apartment at 16 Flagler Street. Not knowing how to read or write, she kept track of her boarders' food supplies by tying each bundle with different colored threads or by marking them with a sign.

She also ran a small candy store at the top of Flagler Street which she opened at dawn to sell sandwiches to her boarders and others on their way to work.

Angela Michelle was six feet tall, taller than most of the men of Flagler Street. Her comical nature made her popular; her native wisdom made her respected. She called everyone, friend and stranger alike, "Cara Mia." She danced a memorable tarantella *at summer block parties.*

She was a strong woman, so strong, they say, that once, hearing there was free firewood at an estate a mile away, she walked there, hoisted a six-foot log on top of her head and, hands on hips, marched back to Flagler Street. After all, the wood was free, wasn't it?

Clarence Gill

Italian mothers with their children at Cauldwell Playground. **1905.**

The kitchen was the heart of the home. Mothers fed their families on pasta, beans, garden vegetables, homemade bread and fish on Fridays.

They were strict, loving, volatile and seldom outtalked. The long wooden spoon that stirred tomato gravy was an extension of a father's authority. Mothers wielded the spoon or the stick suddenly and with force; a child could not hide from its long arm.

Family feeling was extended to the entire community. Children were expected to address all elders as "Zio" ("Uncle") or "Zia" ("Aunt")—or else be reprimanded twice; once by their own parents and again by the offended "relative."

Despite skimpy budgets, immigrant mothers nourished their families with love.

Every Friday night mothers cleared long wooden tables to mix dough for the large cartwheel loaves of bread that would feed their families for the next week.

"As a kid when I came home from school," said ***Louis Goduto,*** "I'd say in Italian, 'Mom, how about a slice of bread?' She'd go and cut me a big slice, about so long," he motioned with his hands, "and I'd put fatback or bacon grease on it."

Early Saturday morning, women put the dough in pans, covered it with a damp towel and balanced it on their heads to walk down the street to Verrilli's bakery. Leonardo Verrilli and his wife, Antonia, let Italian housewives bake their bread at a small fee while the ovens were cooling off.

"I remember my mother making bread at home," Mr. Goduto continued. "I used to call them 'cartwheels,' those big round loaves that weighed five or six pounds apiece."

The women put pieces of paper in the dough to identify their loaves. Later in the day, around noon, children brought the bread back in wagons, having recognized their family's bread by its unique marker. The bread was kept all week long, covered with sheets to keep it fresh.

Every Friday the "fish man" arrived early in the morning on the train from New York City. He pushed his wagon of fresh fish up Flagler Street, followed by an army of hungry cats. Housewives anticipated his arrival because there was no place to buy fresh fish in Morristown.

Children followed the "fish man," too. "Some of the kids used to follow him on Flagler Street, shouting, 'Your fish stinks!'" recalled ***Jim Costanzo*** with a laugh. "They thought they were funny. What he yelled back was unprintable."

Flour was bought in 100-pound sacks which later became sheets and itchy underwear. Women soaked the coarse material for days to soften it, then sewed the sacks together to make sheets; four-and-a-half flour bags made

Women working at the Rosevere Pants factory. **Water Street, 1904.**

one sheet.

Mr. Goduto also remembered his mother "taking empty flour and sugar bags and going down to Pocahontas Lake to pick out a spot for washing. She spread those bags on stones and soaked them with water, rubbing them to get the flour and sugar emblems off. Then she rinsed the bags thoroughly, carried them home, put them in boiling water and scrubbed them on a washboard to get rid of the printing. Later she made towels, bedsheets and pillowcases out of them."

Tomatoes grown in the backyard were made into tomato *conserva* (paste) which became the base for countless dishes. ***John Chiappa*** described how his mother made tomato paste outdoors.

"She cooked them until they were pretty thick and spread them on flat boards so the sun could shine on them all day while the water ran off. When all the water was gone, she packed the paste in raisins with olive oil to keep it from going bad. Some was made with hot peppers, some was just the normal tomato paste. My mother also canned many, many quarts of tomatoes, seeds and all; we used them for stew and things like that."

"I didn't like it when Grandma made *conserva*," said ***Mrs. Rose Vigilante,*** "because we had to stand near the boards with large cloths and keep waving them to keep the flies away. Later on my Grandmother bought a machine that skinned tomatoes and separated seeds."

Besides tomatoes and bread, dandelion greens, gathered for salad in the early spring, escarole and beans, fried peppers, homemade sausage and *pasta fagiola* (macaroni and beans) were familiar foods.

"They lived better than people do today," said Mr. Chiappa. "The only way you can live today is if you got the dollar in your pocket and you go to the store and get what you need. In those days, they put away what they needed and when they needed something, they went down to the basement and got it. Or they resold it."

In addition to taking care of her own family, the Italian housewife took in boarders. She charged each boarder $3 a month to cook and clean and thus supplemented her husband's average daily wage of a dollar a day. She took in as many boarders as space and her strength would allow and thus doubled the family income without leaving home.

She also doubled her influence: The woman who earned money earned new power not possible in Italy. She was the banker who handled the money. Shrewdly, she saved as much as she could whenever she could, towards the purchase of a dream—to buy a home or, with her husband, to open a business.

When a family took in boarders, it changed everyone's life. Rooms were tiny and families were large. Making space for more people meant everyone was crowded into

Italian women on a Cauldwell Playground outing to Coney Island. **c. 1925.**

two bedrooms, leaving the third bedroom free.

That room was cleared of furniture, and beds were placed as close together as possible. The number of boarders was decided by the number of beds that could fit into a room. The average was seven.

Washing clothes for the laborers was no small job. ***Mrs. Minnie Cherello*** recalled her mother-in-law's long hours of scrubbing workclothes by hand, into "all hours of the night."

Men bought their own food, spending $2 a month if they bought their pasta in 20-pound bundles. "Our boarders never seemed to eat out of one pot," said Mrs. Cherello. "We had about a dozen different things to cook on the stove. Some wanted beans, someone else wanted this or that. And we had to cook it all.

"We kept the food down in the cold cellar. All those women used to work and cook for those boarders for $3 a month. They worked hard, but they never complained. Who were they going to complain to?"

Mrs. Frances DeBrito in front of the family store. **Flagler and Water Streets, Morristown.**

Mrs. Celeste Antonaccio. **1925.**

"Zia" Lucia Mainiero with her grandson, Joseph Mainiero (standing), and granddaughter, Carmella Nodoro, in front of her candy store on Flagler Street. **1932.**

The Italian housewife took in as many boarders as space and her strength would allow. Zia Lucia took in 23.

The building where Zia Lucia kept 23 boarders in the basement. **c. 1915.**

"It amazes me that my mother worked all the time and never squawked. She could have been dead tired, working day and night. There were nine children in our family. She really had to work hard to raise us."

Nicholas DeNunzio

Mrs. Rocco (Theodora) Mastrafano in her garden. **c. 1935.**

Rosina Romano with her daughter, Julia Parella, and granddaughter, Pauline.

Samuel and Ethel Berkowitz (front row, right) with employees at their factory, the Gloria Coat Company, off Abbott Avenue. **Morristown, 1952.**

Josephine Baldino, secretary to Worrall Mountain, Associate Justice of the New Jersey Supreme Court.

Mrs. (Vito) Anna Sylvester with her children in the family grocery store. **Spring Street. 1932.**

Joseph and Henry Morandi with their niece, Fanny Cattano (Manning), in front of the building they owned.

Mrs. Erminia Costanzo in front of the family store. **Water Street. 1935.**

Lucille Grande on her engagement to Cosimo DeBellonia. **1910.**

"When an Italian woman has a daughter, she says, 'This is going to be for my daughter when she gets married,' and she buys a sheet. Or a towel. She puts it in a trunk. When you are five or six years old, you have a start on a dowry.

"The Italian mother prepares the trunk all the time her daughter is growing up. People couldn't buy everything all at one time; they didn't have that kind of money. By the time you get married, everything is ready for you."

Minnie Pisciotto

Mrs. (Frederick) Tina Camisa with her son, Jack. **1909.**

Filomena Orlando with her grandson, Benjamin ("Biago") Signorelli.

Mrs. (Patsy) Maria Parella with her granddaughters, Rose and Marie Pirone.

Four generations of Pennucci women: (standing) Maria (Corea), Pauline Pennucci, Repy (Hattersby) and Susan (Hattersby). **1960.**

Lucia DeNunzio's 85th birthday party. **1935.**

Mrs. (Leopold) Anna Mischiara at the beach. **1937.**

Mrs. (James) Filomena DeRuggiero.

Mrs. (Frederick) Mary Sandelli (center) celebrating her 10th wedding anniversary with her girlfriends. **1931.**

Members of the Victory Club during World War II.

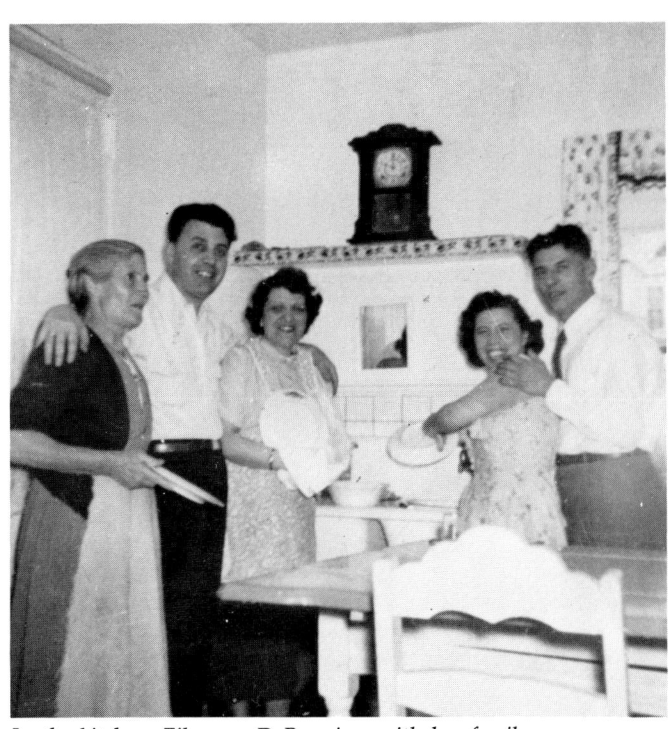

In the kitchen: Filomena DeRuggiero with her family.

Joseph Perrucci with his grandmother, Christine (Tremallo) Cutter.

Mrs. (William) Ida Ferraro with son George.

Maria Meola with her grandchildren.

The Joseph Andresano family. **c. 1935.**

Genevieve (Trullo) DeChiaro with her sister, Jessie (r), and son. **1942.**

Vincenza Ciannello with her children, Mary, Angelo and Margaret. **1916.**

Michael Levato (front) and Nicholas DeNunzio (back) laying brick for Bamberger's Store. **Morristown, 1948.**

IV. From the Ground Up: Men at Work

"My father came to America in 1899. He had read an ad in an Italian newspaper that advertised jobs for railroad laborers in America. When he landed on Ellis Island, he didn't know where he was going to work until he was met by railroad recruiters. He and some other men were taken to the Delaware Lackawanna Railroad Station in Hoboken, New Jersey. They went to Boonton on the train and from Boonton to Denville.

"Pop and three other fellows were living in a shanty. They didn't have any facilities. Some of the other shanties had as much as 30 men living in them. They slept on bunk beds. They cooked their meals on outdoor stoves and ate outdoors. They had it hard, but they didn't mind.

"Their only amusement was playing cards or bocci. *Sometimes they would ride a bike to Rockaway or Denville, three miles away.*

"My father worked on the railroad for $1.10 a day for 10 hours work, that's 11¢ an hour.

"When he had enough money, he sent for my mother."

John Chiappa

Frank Stirone and Thomas Landi digging a foundation.

It was a shock to realize how much money a man needed to live in America. It was ironic, considering that it was the opportunity to earn money that had attracted the immigrant to America.

"In America I made the Sign of the Cross every morning to pray that I worked and bought food that day," said ***Anthony DeLorenzo.*** "Here you needed money every day. In Italy we cut wheat, oats, grain, we had chickens, sheep and goats, so we had food and didn't have to worry about buying any. Here we had to squeeze the dollar and save money."

Here, too, was the unfamiliar burden of paying rent. The wealthy landowner no longer took care, however meagerly, of the Italian family. This was the price of trading serfdom for freedom.

To ***Joseph Andresano,*** it was worth it. Life in Italy, when he left in 1913, was "misery." He was 14 years old.

"I didn't get enough bread for a meal over there," he said, "I worked for nothing, or for 10¢ a day, from four o'clock in the morning until eight o'clock at night.

"Over here I could earn more than a dollar a day.

"You had to go some to spend a dollar in those days. You could buy something for a nickel, another thing for a dime, that's all. Bread was 5¢ a loaf, a pair of shoes was $3, a new suit, $10.

"And when you got a raise, a raise of a dime, that was big. Are you kidding? Ten cents was 10 cents. You could buy two loaves of bread with that.

"Whenever you asked a foreman for a job, you had to tip your hat," he continued. "The way to do it was to tip the hat and ask politely, 'Do you have a job for me?' If the boss was good, he found one for you."

Sam D'Angelo remembered that his early jobs were strenuous. He thought back to the job that required him to unload a carload of cement. "Blood used to come out of my fingers. But we were used to working hard then. Not like today. They go to work, get $10 an hour, push a button and think they're working."

Joseph Dandino recalled that his father's railroad job was "tough work, digging, the heavy rails and ties and all that. I remembered Zio Crescenzo, he was stooped over from loading cars all the time. Men got that way, too, from tamping railroad ties."

In the first two decades of the 20th century, trenches were needed as indoor plumbing became available and sewage pipes were installed. The men of Flagler Street were readily hired to dig ditches.

It was a job requiring energy and stamina. A man in a trench could work all day and hardly see the sky. Some trenches were 10 feet deep, with platforms built into the side wall. Men at the bottom shoveled dirt up to the platform where another crew threw it up to ground level.

Tony Loia dug ditches for $1.50 a day. He was 17 when he left Tocco Audio, Italy, near Benevento, where many of Flagler Street's Italians had come from.

"I came to America in 1913. It took me 21 days to come over on the boat, from May 21 to June 11, and cost 100

Construction workers on the job.

lire. That's $20. At the time it was a lot of money. I had more lire with me in case I didn't get a job. I had $5 to cover me.

"It was hard for me to leave my parents," he said, "but I was ready to come. I wanted to make money here, to buy property. My mother and father never came over."

He tried working in the city first, but after an accident on his factory job he decided to take his uncle's advice and look for a farm job in Morristown. He found work tending chickens on an estate and later dug ditches for a water company.

During World War I he served in the U.S. Army. After the war, he went back to the ditches. "I was the boss that time, when we dug ditches to lay pipe." A crew of 14 worked for him.

He became a contractor without knowing how to read or write. "I learned the numbers," he explained.

The necessity of adapting quickly to any situation was part of survival.

"My grandfather was a steward on a ship," ***Tommy Rago*** related. "He'd work his way over, stay until he ran out of money, then work his way back. He'd stay a year or two, that was his way of life. His main objective was to get his kids here, to live the American way." When he finally settled down on Flagler Street around 1910, he found work at the Morris County Golf Club.

"He wasn't a caddy, he was shrewd," his grandson said fondly. "Anything to make a dollar. He picked up golf balls and sold them back to the guys who hit them into the woods. Whenever he did caddy and someone hit a ball into the rough, he would say he couldn't find it. A couple of days later he went back, dug it up and sold it to someone else."

Frank DiPrimo's father came to Flagler Street from Ginosa, Italy, next to Benevento, in 1903.

"He was a hod carrier," his son recalled. "He worked in Mendham and lived in Morristown in a shack with four or five men. I used to hear him talk about it, how they'd eat beans and walk five miles back and forth to work each day.

"The shacks were little places with just a pipe in the roof to let the air out. They had no toilet, no sink. Just a pot stove and a mattress to sleep on and a blanket. They did their own cooking, mostly beans. In the winter when they didn't have shoes or boots, they tied sacks on their feet to walk to work in the snow."

The working "aristocrats" of Flagler Street were the stonecutters and masons whose skill with mortar and trowel raised stately buildings around Morris County, notably St. Peter's Episcopal Church, the Morristown Public Library, St. Elizabeth's College and the Community Theater.

Masons were better paid than laborers, and their work was admired and respected. They held themselves apart from men who dug ditches for a living.

Anthony Cherello described Sunday morning gatherings around 1910 when the distinction between mason and laborer was clearly drawn. These gatherings were

Charles (back) and Joseph (front) Cattano in their barber shop on Washington Street. **c. 1925.**

held at the top of Flagler Street, in front of Bontempo's and Mainiero's, in a small area known as "Fifth Avenue."

"I used to see men gather in front of Bontempo's Store and the Mainiero Building," Mr. Cherello recalled. "Mr. Bozzi, Mr. Petrillo, Mr. Bontempo, Mr. Maggio and the other masons would get into discussions about their work and the topics of the day.

"The laborers would stand alongside them, in a little group next to the masons, and they would discuss their work and their problems. All the men in both groups were dressed in their best clothes, smoking cigars and pipes.

"They never interrupted each other's conversations.

"The masons stood in one circle, the laborers in another. There was a caste system. The masons regarded themselves as tradesmen, superior because they had a trade. The workers were looked down upon as *zappadore* (laborers) and beneath them.

"Masons, when they worked on a building, didn't ask for bricks and cement to be brought up to them. They demanded, they spoke with authority and the laborers obeyed."

The Italian laborer changed Morristown. He hauled the stones and the bricks that eventually became new buildings uptown. He dug the ditches that brought the pipes that modernized Morristown. He laid the railroad tracks that linked the town to the outside world.

In the process, he changed himself.

Employees of the Bontempo-D'Annunzio Construction Company at the site of the Morristown Jewish Community Center.

Salvatore Bontempo and Jessie D'Annunzio with their wedding party. **1921.**

Cutting stone during construction of St. Elizabeth's College in Convent, New Jersey. (Mike Sandelli is in foreground.) **c. 1925.**

St. Peter's Episcopal Church in Morristown nearing completion. **1907.**

Italian stonecutters and masons gave the finished church its stately appearance. (Sturgis Brothers Company.)

Dedication of the Morristown Jewish Community Center. **1927.**

The Morristown Jewish Community Center. **1982.** *(Photograph by James V. Costanzo, Jr.)*

Luigi Squerzi laying brick at Mt. Hope School. **1931.**

At work. **c. 1950.**

Taking a break.

Al Ciampaglia and Louis Desimone.

The 50th anniversary dinner of the bricklayers' union. **1942.**

Members of the hod carriers union greet former U.S. Senator Harrison Williams and his wife during their anniversary dinner. (Joseph Perrucci, local delegate, is to the right.)

Carmine Petrone, fireman.

The "Whitewings," Morristown's Sanitation Department: Messrs. Nicola, Rago, Mainiero, Gervasio, Kilkenny, Orlando and Mariatto. **Photographed on Morristown Green, 1913.** *(Courtesy of* The Daily Record, *Morristown.)*

Leonard Palminteri (r), owner, in his barber shop with George Ferraro, (l), his employee. **1920's.**

Vito Magestro, Joe Dandino and friend riding a "gandy dancer" on the railroad tracks in Morristown.

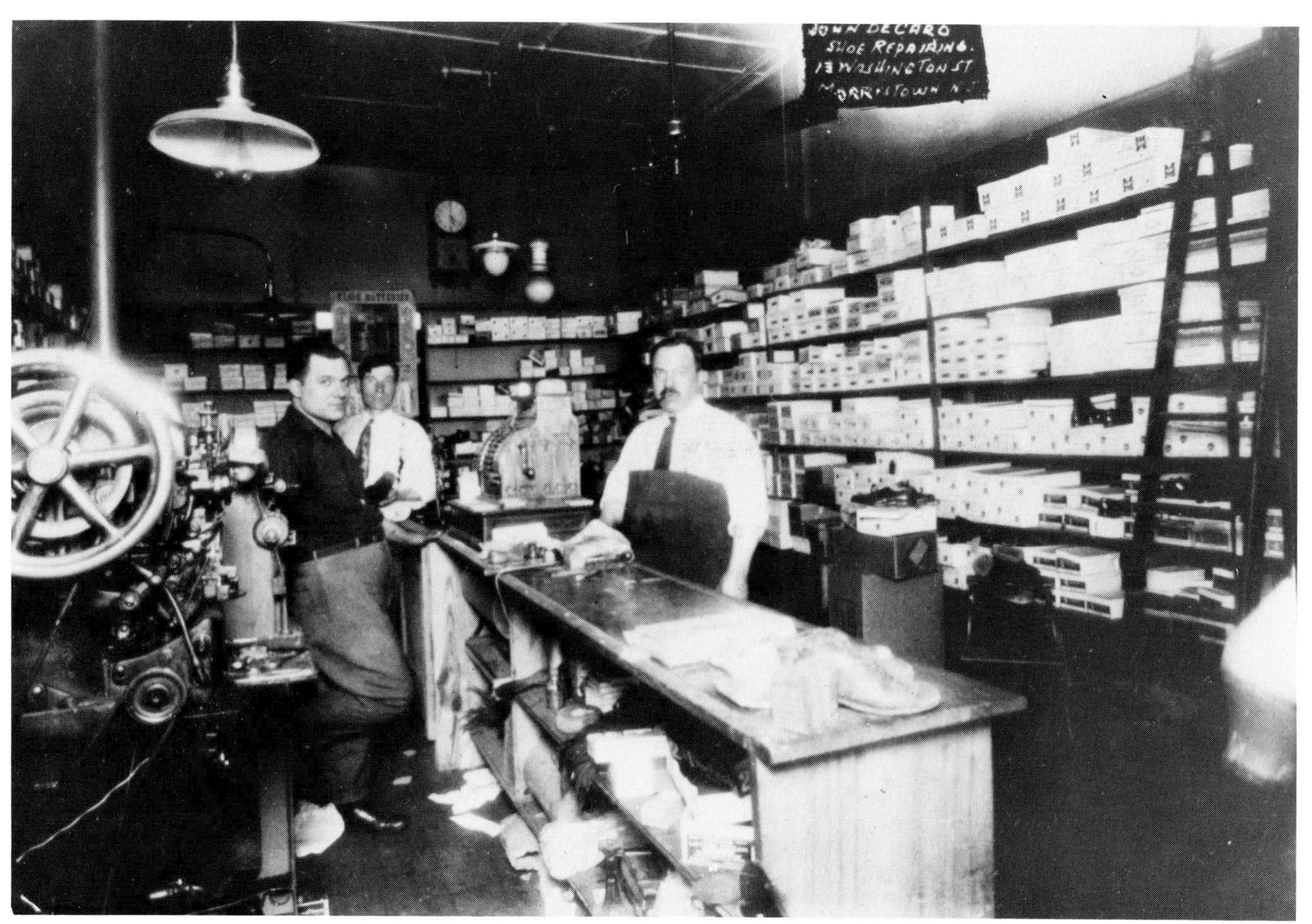

John DeCaro in his Washington Street shoe repair shop.

Leonard Mainiero (r) in his restaurant on Washington Street.

Tony D'Angelo and Frank Goduto behind the bar in their tavern on Flagler Street. **1934.**

Outside the Campus Market on South Street (l-r): Emilio Caravaggio, Vito Cifrese (owner) and Dominick Ciocca. **1922.**

Michael Rubino in his South Street shoe shop, which specialized in handmade shoes for Morristown's wealthy class. **c. 1930.**

Vincent Dalcanzo in his shoe repair shop on Washington Street. **1948.**

Big Chief Market, South Street: Vito Bitondo, Joe Pennucci and Pat Soranno. **c. 1939.**

Tony Pennucci at his parent's candy store on Evergreen Avenue.

John Morandi with his grandson, Anthony Gerardi. **c. 1936.**

V. Survival: Everybody's Business

"Once I had three jobs, and I was still in grammar school. I took care of Mr. Dana's furnace on Speedwell Avenue, he had a meat shop down by the railroad station. In the morning I shook the furnace, threw coal on the fire and sometimes sifted the ashes. At night, about 10:30, I banked the fire. After that I went down to Dominic and Jeanette's Restaurant on Water Street to cook hamburgers until a quarter to 12.

"Besides that, I got a job in a coat factory and right after school I went there to make buttonholes on the machine. I got $1.50 for the furnace job; $2.50 from Dominic; and $3 from the coat factory. I made $7 a week from the three jobs and was 13 years old. I got home at midnight, and did my homework at school or in the restaurant when I had time. All in all, I gave my mother about $500 from my earnings."

Tony Galdi

Louise and Frank Galdieri (back) in their grocery store on Morris Street, with sons Louis and Carmine (l) and partners James and Salvatore DeChiaro (r). **1929.**

The only way families on Flagler Street were able to survive during those early hard years was if everyone contributed to the family income. Children often began working at eight or nine years old.

Any money earned—even if it was only pennies—was turned over to the mother. A youngster whose father owned a store on Flagler Street was expected to report for work at the store immediately after school. Women worked in nearby factories including Beckman's Pants Factory, Bricker's Umbrella Factory and Goodman's Blouse and Underwear Factory.

Luke Soranno remembered his mother pulling weeds at the Morris County Golf Club.

"Back around 1919, my mother and some of the Flagler Street mothers worked pulling weeds out of the greens at the Morris County Golf Club. Gus Donofrio was the greenskeeper. He had a truck that came and picked up the ladies. His mother worked there, also Mrs. Galdi, Angela Michelle and others. Some of the daughters when they were 15 also worked on the greens during the summer." Women also swept early morning dew off the greens, using long-handled sticks, and picked weeds at Rochelle's Farm in Mendham.

Young girls like ***Jennie Innacola*** cleaned houses for well-to-do families.

"On Saturdays I would clean Mrs. Hirsch's house on Hillary Avenue, six rooms for 10¢. When she raised me to 25¢, I gave 15¢ to my mother and kept a dime to buy ice cream. I enjoyed working for Mrs. Hirsch because she gave me Dugan's bread and cakes, and I saved on lunch. It was a treat. I was 12 years old."

Daughters often left school at 13 or 14 to take jobs in a factory or at Morey La Rue's laundry.

Mrs. Rose Vigilante went to work in 1910.

"I had my first job when I was 13, in Morey LaRue's Laundry, earning $4.50 or $5 a week. I worked six days a week, all day Saturday, from seven in the morning to six at night. The Irish girls worked upstairs on the street level, ironing the rich people's fancy clothes. We Italian girls worked in the basement, doing the flat work, folding pillow cases, handkerchiefs and sheets.

"After six months I went to work at Beckman's Pants Factory where I made $9 a week.

"One day I took fried pepper sandwiches to work with me, wrapped in paper. The peppers were fried in olive oil, and the grease leaked through the paper. The Irish girls asked me to exchange sandwiches with them because they said mine smelled so good. I said to them, 'Who wants to switch? All you've got is peanut butter and jelly.'"

Mrs. Erminia Costanzo also went to work at a young age. "The first job I had was in 1904 when I was 14 years old, sewing pants. When I went to get the job, I was so thin my mother gave me something to give me a shape so I would look older, and I wore a long dress and high heels. I got the job because I told my boss I was 16.

"When I first went there I made $2 a week on piecework. I had to learn how to work the electric sewing machine and I was scared, so afraid of them. There were two workrooms, one where the men worked cutting out pants from patterns, and another room where about 30 women, mostly Italian, were sewing. We couldn't talk

Cifrese's Vegetable Store on Speedwell Avenue. **1921.**

while we were working because we were on piecework, trying to finish as many pants as we could. I never lost a day's work while I was there and when I left to get married, I was the highest paid girl in the factory; I got $10.75 a week.

"I gave my mother my salary in an envelope to make her happy," Mrs. Costanzo said.

"But I had a little arrangement. I got my boss to give me a little bit of change in my hand. That's what I kept for myself. I gave that to my uncle to save for me until I got married. I spent a nickel a day on ice cream and that was all."

Flagler Street's sons looked for jobs at an early age. They sold newspapers, set up pins in bowling alleys, delivered groceries, cut lawns and shoveled snow.

John Chiappa recalled his days as a newsboy for the hometown newspaper, *The Daily Record.*

"In 1911, when I was eight years old, I remember my mother giving me a nickel. I bought eight *Daily Records* and went out and sold them. After I'd sold them, I'd go back and get another nickel's worth. I probably made 6¢ for the whole time. That was a big profit, 6¢.

"Sometimes we used to make money hitching horses in front of the post office next to the newspaper building. Guys would ask us to hold their horse for them. We'd get a penny or two, which was a lot of money to us. Better than selling papers if you got enough of those jobs."

So many boys from Flagler Street sold newspapers after school that there was a rush towards *The Daily Record* building to see who could be on the street first with that day's edition. Steady customers were found in uptown stores and taverns.

"We had to hustle," Mr. Chiappa remembered, "we tried to make money to help our families. There were eight in our family and that 6¢ a day was a help. We made sure we took our pennies home because we knew they were needed."

Tony Elia set up pins in a bowling alley when he was nine years old.

"Everybody those days had to work. There was so little income, all the kids tried to do what odd jobs they could, then give the money to their parents. I made about $4 a week setting up pins. I gave it to my mother, and she gave me back 25¢ out of the $4. Then she wanted to know what I was going to do with the quarter!

"But we never squawked. We were helping out. That was a little bit more money in the kitty. She kept it all in a big tin.

"I remember in later years as we kids grew older and got better jobs, we all pitched in and gave up our pay and finally in a short time we knocked off the mortgage on our house. At the old man's rate it would have taken 50 years."

Mr. Chiappa's first summer job was in 1914, when he worked as a water boy on a construction job. He was 10 years old.

"I carried water to the laboring men. Gangs were spread far apart; you had to go from one gang to another. In addition, I had to light all the lanterns at night, take them down in the morning, clean them and fill them with kerosene."

The following winter he delivered groceries for Frank

Lucio Tartaglia (center) with his son Anthony (seated) and employees in his tailor shop on Speedwell Avenue. **1921.**

Petrozzo's store. "I used to make deliveries on a sled, bags of flour weighed 100 pounds each, stuff like that. When I delivered to 16 Flagler Street where four or five families lived, I had to make two trips. I could pick up 100 pounds of flour like it was nothing."

Caddying at the Morris County Golf Club was another way to earn money in the summer, although boys did not linger once their job was done. "We got back to Flagler Street in a hurry," recalled ***R. Sar Mischiara.*** "We either ran home or hitched a ride on a trolley. If we took too much time a policeman would tell us we were loitering."

Stores were family businesses, with wives working alongside their husbands and children growing up in the business.

"My first and only job was in my brother-in-law's barber shop," said ***Pat Francis.*** "I worked there after school for nine years, swept up the shop and combed hair. I used to stand right alongside my brother-in-law, Lou (Donnamaria), and watch how he cut hair. I got 25¢ a week for pay. It was my job to keep the place clean. I had to pick up the spittoon, dump it out and brush it with sand. Every day.

"On Sunday, we lit the fire at 6:30 in the morning, using wood and coal. I had a pan of water on the stove ready for shaving. We worked all day Saturday, from 7 a.m. until 1:30 a.m. At the time a haircut was 25¢ and a shave was 15¢."

The Sagarese brothers, Joseph and Robert, reported to their father's plumbing business every afternoon after school.

"In those days, you helped," said ***Robert Sagarese.*** "During vacation you didn't play ball, you had to work, learn a trade. I was about 12 when I started to help in 1908. We used to help my father carry pipe and materials to the job. We had no horse and wagon then. Had to carry everything."

In the 1920's, ***Tommy Rago*** got up at four o'clock in the morning to help out in his father's shoe repair business on Speedwell Avenue.

"We got up that early because we used to solicit shoe repairs up in Mount Freedom, which was a summer resort. My father had a way about him—he'd make me think it was something enjoyable, to go to work. Believe me it was, the way he put it.

"'Let's go to the diner, have a cup of coffee and some breakfast and go to work.' That's what he'd say. And we'd be working from four o'clock in the morning until nine o'clock at night. That's the way he made a buck in the summertime.

"We'd go to all the hotels and bungalows in Mount Freedom, pick up shoes, solicit shoes for repair and deliver them the next week."

In all things, thrift came before prosperity. "We used everything," Tony Elia recalled.

"For example, we didn't throw any part of a chicken away. My mother would stick the chicken in the neck, turn it upside down and let the blood go into a dish. She would fry the blood, and we would have blood sandwiches with salt and pepper. We didn't waste anything. Used to eat the feet and everything. I think the only thing she threw away was the head."

Tony Galdi added, "I get a kick out of garbage pails

Carmen and Angelina Monaco with their children and grandchildren. **c. 1925.**

today. When we were kids we didn't have garbage pails because we had nothing to put in them. We ate everything and threw away nothing."

In the early 1920's, when times were very hard, buying food had to wait until money was earned, ***Peter Cattano*** recalled.

"One day my Pop was just leaving to go to work in his barber shop on Washington Street when my mother told him to give me a dollar.

"She said to me, 'Buy three dozen eggs and two quarts of milk and don't forget to bring me back the change.'

"My father turned around to her and said, in Italian, 'I haven't earned a dollar yet. Wait till I go to the shop and make some money first.'"

Sons took immense pleasure when the money they contributed to a household made new purchases possible.

Ralph Cangelosi remembered that in the 1930's he and his brother Jules found jobs in a General Motors plant in Linden, a few miles from Morristown.

"We each earned $26 a week, and each of us gave our mother $20 because it made her happy. We kept $6 for ourselves and with that money together we bought Mom her first washing machine. Before that she had washed clothes by hand. Later on, still from that $6, we bought her a refrigerator."

Italian mothers were also ingenious. Mrs. Mischiara, for example, once paid a dentist's bill for her children back in 1910 by giving the doctor a good supply of her homemade tomato sauce.

Nicholas DeNunzio looked back on those early days with admiration.

"It amazes me that my mother worked all the time and never squawked. She could have been dead tired, working day and night. There were nine children in our family. She really had to work hard to raise us."

The grand old men and women of Flagler Street are remembered today with fondness and affection by their children, themselves now growing old.

"They were great, they had love in their eyes," recalled Mrs. Costanzo. "They were powerful men and women."

"I wish we had those old times again," said ***John Stirone.*** "Now we're all out for ourselves, each going his own way and not getting together with families. We don't have the time. We're all better off financially, but there's something missing."

Officers of the Sons of Italy. **c. 1922.**

"Like the famiglia *and the church, the mutal aid society was an important component of the Italian-American community. Dedicated to mutual aid and protection in case of sickness, death or other misfortune, its membership was recruited exclusively from the* paese. *It not only constituted the heart of the* contadino's *social life in America, but it was their continuing point of contact with the town or* paese *from which they came. The federation of many of these and other societies into the Order of the Sons of Italy in America was a natural sequence . . ."*

Dr. Francesco Cordasco

Sons of Italy outing in Long Branch, New Jersey. **1920's.**

Members of the Morristown Columbian Club. **c. 1960.**

Joseph and Carmella Chiappa (center) with their children.

Gus Donofrio (r), greenskeeper at the Morris County Golf Club, with his godson, Joseph Antonaccio. **c. 1925.**

Anthony Elia with his parents, Mr. and Mrs. Sebastiano Elia.

Vincent LaRicci in his tailor shop on Speedwell Avenue. **1920's.**

Vincent LaRicci on his wedding day to Regina Barone.

The Maiettas, Panellis and Sparanos welcome home John Maietta (standing, r) on leave during World War II.

The Ubertaccio family (l-r): Ralph, Peter, Frances, Angelo, Nunzia, Rocco, Ann, Emmanuel, Ignace. **1947.**

Tony DeNunzio, Nick Parella, Tony Romano and Dominick Bontempo on River Street. **1917.**

Neighborhood House boys. **c. 1940.**

(standing): William Ferraro, (unidentified), Ernest Gioglio, Antonio Maggio; (seated) Vito Palagonia.

The Sagarese brothers: (standing) Joseph, Robert, Salvatore, Michael; (kneeling) Frank and Alfred.

Pietro and Filomena Giordano with their daughter-in-law, Mrs. John Giordano.

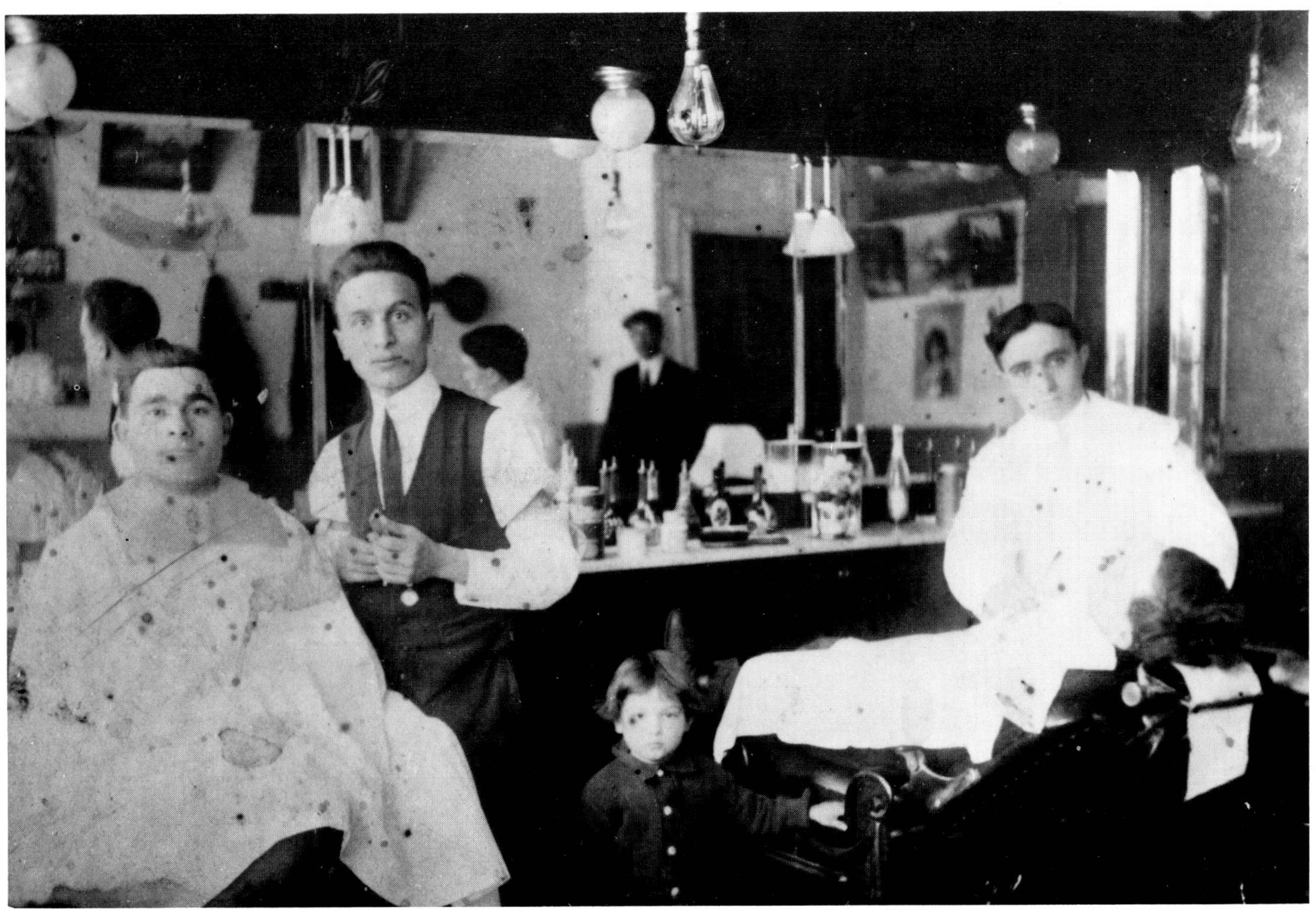

Vincent DiFalco (left) in his barber shop at 10 Flagler Street, with customer Angelo Traetto. **c. 1910.**

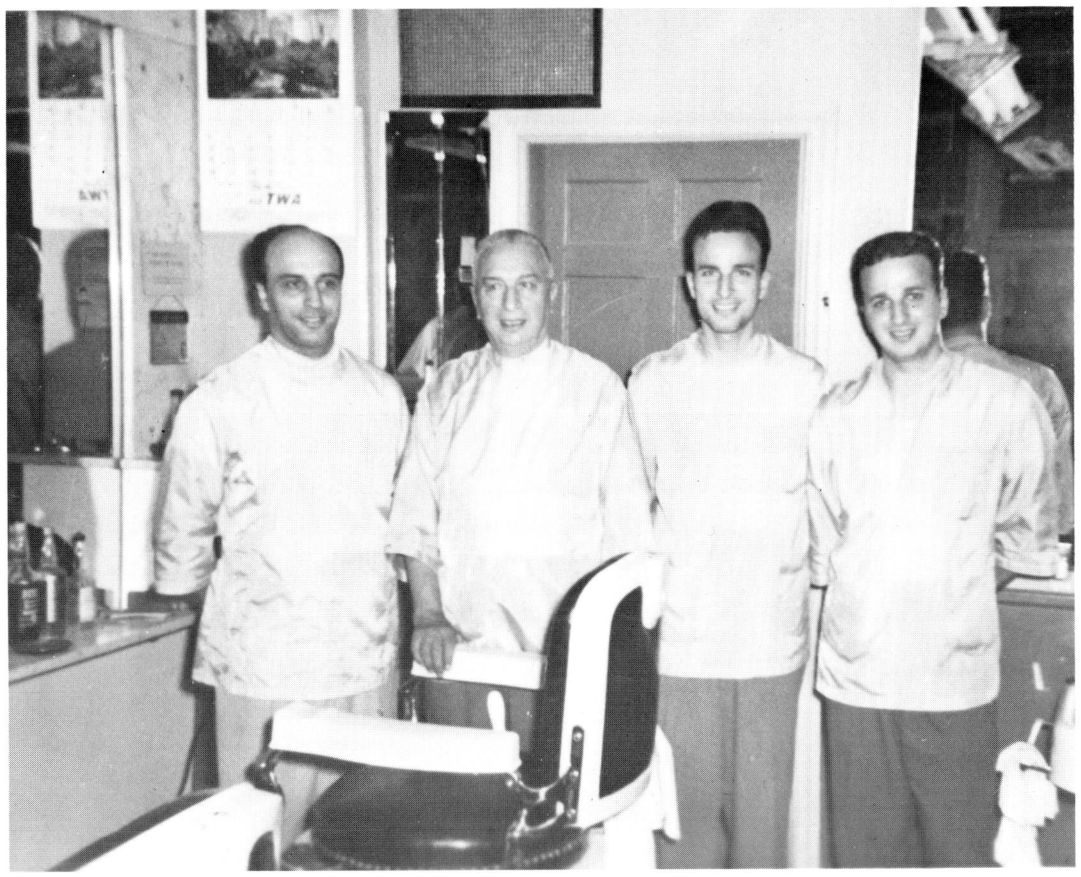

Vincent DiFalco (second, left) with his sons in the family barber shop. **c. 1960.**

Mary Lucia with her children: (standing) Fred, Joe, Florence, Sam, Dan, (seated) Giloroma and Mary. **1955.**

Fedele and Mary Lucia, in their backyard.

Friends gathered at the Donato D'Iorio home on Nicholas Avenue for a party.

Mrs. (John) Madeline Santoro and children.

Dominic and Eurilia Margiotta at home with their children on Hazel Street. **August, 1939.**

Mr. and Mrs. Margiotta with friends. **1938.**

Montescaglioso Club picnic at Forest Lodge in Warren Township, New Jersey. **August, 1958.**

Sons of Italy outing. **c. 1927.**

Officers of the Columbian Club. **c. 1950.**

The Columbian Club's Board of Trustees: (back row) Joseph Masterfano, Anthony Giordano, Liborio Cifrese, William Pagano and Louis Petrone; (front row) Joseph Petrone, Frank Bitondo and Dominick Pisciotto. (Patrick Ninni is absent.) **1982.**

Frank Petrozzo and Mary Verrilli on their wedding day. **October 2, 1910.**

VI. Old World and New: Rituals and Customs

Benedetta Petrozzo thought it was time for her son Frank to get married.

He had been in America for six years, working in Newark and out in San Francisco before coming back to settle in Morristown. He had his own grocery store on Flagler Street next to the Grupelli Flats, but Benedetta felt her 24-year-old son would amount to nothing without a wife. If he wouldn't do anything about it, she would. She was anxious to go back home to Montescaglioso, Italy.

Once she saw healthy, hardworking Mary Verrilli, Benedetta knew this was the girl for her Frank. "You need a wife," she told her son. "I've got to go home soon, and I want to see you married before I go. I have Mary Verrilli in mind for you, she's the baker's daughter."

Frank, who had also seen Mary at work in the bakery, knew she flirted with others. He answered his mother bluntly. "How do you know she wants me? I'll never ask her unless I am sure she will say yes."

Thus encouraged, Benedetta went into action. Her first two attempts failed. Mary sent word through her stepmother that she wasn't interested in marrying Frank—or anyone else for that matter. After all, she was just 15 and already had her eye on a boyfriend.

The first matchmaker Benedetta approached was unsuccessful and the situation became complicated when Mary's family warmed to the idea of her marriage to Frank—but she didn't. On Flagler Street, Frank was considered a good catch. Tempers flared.

The second matchmaker, Carolina Correale, was just as stubborn as Mary: "Wouldn't it be better being married and in your own house?" she asked the girl. Mary relented, agreeing to meet Frank's family first, and then Frank himself, "I will say 'Yes,'" she promised Carolina after several changes of heart.

Frank, busy in his store, didn't know about all this. All he knew was what he had overheard: another young man boasting that he had been promised Mary's hand.

When Frank arrived at the Verrilli home, he was wary.

"I stepped into this house to give you honor," he told Mary's father. "I expect the same."

"And you will get it," replied Leonardo Verrilli.

"Did you promise her to someone else?" Frank came straight to the point.

"No, I did not," thundered Leonardo. Frustrated by four months of his daughter's hemming and hawing, he pointed to Mary standing nearby. "There she is. If she wants you, that's it. If she don't, I can't push it."

On October 2, 1910, Frank and Mary were married on the third floor of Tremallo's Hall at 51 Flagler Street. They named the first of their seven children Benedetta in honor of Frank's patient—and persistent—mother.

Mary Petrozzo

Girls at Cauldwell Playground. **1911.**

Life began and ended at home. Babies were born there, marriages were arranged there, and departed loved ones were bid farewell there.

Familiar customs linked the old world with the new.

There were favorite home remedies to cure a wound or an illness. A headache, for instance, was cured in minutes by dipping the sufferer's head into a pan of water sprinkled with olive oil while Mother chanted in Italian. The blood of a freshly killed rabbit cured a high fever, and "Italian peroxide"—urine—prevented infection. "Pee on it," old women said in Italian when a youngster scraped a knee.

Midwives were an especially comforting presence in an immigrant community because young wives were often separated from their own mothers.

For many years, ***Felice Volpecello***'s mother, Angelina Imparato, was Flagler Street's midwife.

"I think she delivered half the Italian babies in Morristown between 1910 and 1920," said Mrs. Volpecello. "If there were difficult deliveries, she called Dr. Johnson or Dr. Douglas.

"After the baby arrived, she went back to see the newborn and the mother every day for a week. She charged $5, later on, $10." The midwife also brought sheets with her to be cut into diapers for the baby.

"Usually there was no heat in the house except for one little stove in the kitchen," Mrs. Volpecello said, "The babies needed heat, so my mother stayed all night with the infant. She kept the fire going in the stove, put the baby on a cot or chair nearby and opened the oven door so the baby got more heat. Sometimes she turned the baby over to keep it warm."

Healthy babies were born with little commotion and almost no disruption in family routine. Young mothers were known to have a baby in the morning and do a wash in the afternoon. Babies were named for relatives because, as the old saying went, "When I am gone, I will be remembered."

"When an Italian woman had a daughter," ***Minnie Pisciotto*** added, "she says, 'This is going to be for my daughter when she gets married,' and she buys a sheet. Or a towel. She puts it in a trunk. When you are five or six years old, you have a start on a dowry.

"The Italian mother prepares the trunk all the time her daughter is growing up. People couldn't buy things all at one time; they didn't have that kind of money. By the time you get married, everything is ready for you. Linens kept nice and clean."

Later on when a young girl began courting, her parents watched young men suspiciously who came to call. Mothers were strict chaperones: If a courting couple was allowed in a room alone together, Mother was in the next room, listening. Sometimes the rules were even stricter. ***John Stirone*** described the custom.

"When I visited my girl, her aunt would sit opposite us with a yardstick—a three-foot ruler! When she dozed off,

Mrs. Olive Gruber, Neighborhood House instructor, with girls at Cauldwell Playground. **c. 1920.**

pretending to sleep, I would get closer to my girlfriend and naturally try to kiss her. Then the aunt would wake up, wave the ruler at me and say, 'You do that again and I'm going to hit you.'"

In the early days marriages were arranged by matchmakers whose greatest challenge was not in getting two young people together, but in keeping the future bride's father happy. An Italian man wanted his daughter to marry well. "What's he got?" a potential father-in-law would ask about the interested party's financial future.

The weddings that followed negotiations were always happy occasions, though.

"When they had weddings," said ***Pat Ninni,*** "the bride would walk down the stairs (of the apartment building) on the way to the church, and all us kids in the building would be lined up on all three floors to catch the pennies and candies that they threw at the bride.

"The reception was often held in the flats, too, with plenty of food, wine, beer and music. There was enough room for everyone because we used the hallways. It was a happy time."

Weddings were special celebrations, but so were everyday events.

"We had block dances, with fellows playing the guitar and mandolin," he added. "Angela Michelle used to fascinate me, always dancing the *tarantella,* always with a hat on."

Homemade wine, always present on special occasions, was also part of everyday ritual.

Tony Galdi described how his father made wine in the cellar, stored it in gallon jugs and kept it under lock and key.

"He took a pan like the ones you wash clothes in and filled it with water, and put it on a little carpet. You'd walk up to the carpet, rinse and wash your feet and step into a half barrel. You'd throw six or eight or 10 boxes of grapes in there and stomp on them. A wooden half-barrel, that's what he used to crush the grapes in. He would stomp them. What they didn't crush with their feet they'd crush in their hands. We didn't have one of those crushers. Maybe one person in the neighborhood had one, and he lent it to everybody."

When relatives got together, parties went on all night, John Stirone remembered.

"Back in the 20's, in the summers, it was nothing for 25 or 30 of our relatives to visit our aunt and uncle who lived in the Grupelli Flats on Flagler Street. We'd bring a lot of food and vegetables and fruit. Since there wasn't enough room inside, me and my sisters and cousins, we all slept on mattresses on the open porch."

Holidays were festive times when families celebrated being together and forgot their grievances.

"Holidays were big in our family," ***Tony Elia*** said. "Everybody, regardless of whether there had been arguments or not, would get together on holidays, all the children, everyone.

Msgr. John J. Sheerin with the eighth grade graduating class of St. Margaret's Grammar School. **1940.**

"We sat around the table with my father at one end and my mother at the other. All the children, regardless of what arguments they had had with our parents during the year, would go up and kiss first the hand of my mother and then my father. That was one of the things we had to do. Then we would sit down and eat for hours."

Religious holidays were marked by reverence and respect, recalled ***Louis Goduto.***

"Christmas and Easter were our happy days. We used to go visiting house to house. My mother put leaves in the table so 20 people could sit down for dinner. We had all kinds of food: fish, vegetables, meats, grapes, stuffed peppers, artichokes, wine and desserts. My father bought pastries from Ferrara's in New York."

For many years the Andresano flat was spectacularly decorated at Christmastime. The memory is still a vivid one for Mr. Andresano.

"On Christmas Day my father put bulbs, a Christmas tree and pictures of the Infant Jesus, the Blessed Mother, Saint Joseph and the Three Wise Men on the porch of our flat on the first floor. Papa had a procession up to Tremallo's Hall with people carrying the pictures of Jesus, Mary, St. Joseph and the Three Wise Men, and people from the neighborhood came to watch. On Christmas night, the lights were turned on. It was beautiful and every year we did the same thing."

Like other customs, religion and faith were first learned at home. St. Margaret's Church was a short walk from Flagler Street, but in the early years the Italians felt uncomfortable there. They stood or sat on folding chairs in the back of the sanctuary, behind the Irish parishioners who sat comfortably in family pews.

Family prayers were quiet times, recalled ***Pat Leccese.*** "At night, Mom would sit on a chair and teach us how to pray. We'd all sit on the floor around her—my brothers Jimmy and Donald, my sister Julia and me. Mom would teach us in Italian how to say the Lord's Prayer. When my father told us how Jesus was crucified, I could see tears coming from my little brother's eyes."

Groundbreaking ceremony for a new rectory at St. Margaret's. **1937.**

Members of the Montescaglioso Club honor a departed friend. **Assumption Church, Maple Avenue, Morristown.**

Marietta Russomanno and Lucio Tartaglia on their wedding day. **1917.**

Frank and Mary (Verrilli) Petrozzo with their children and grandchildren.

Angelina Imparato, Flagler Street's midwife in the 1920's.

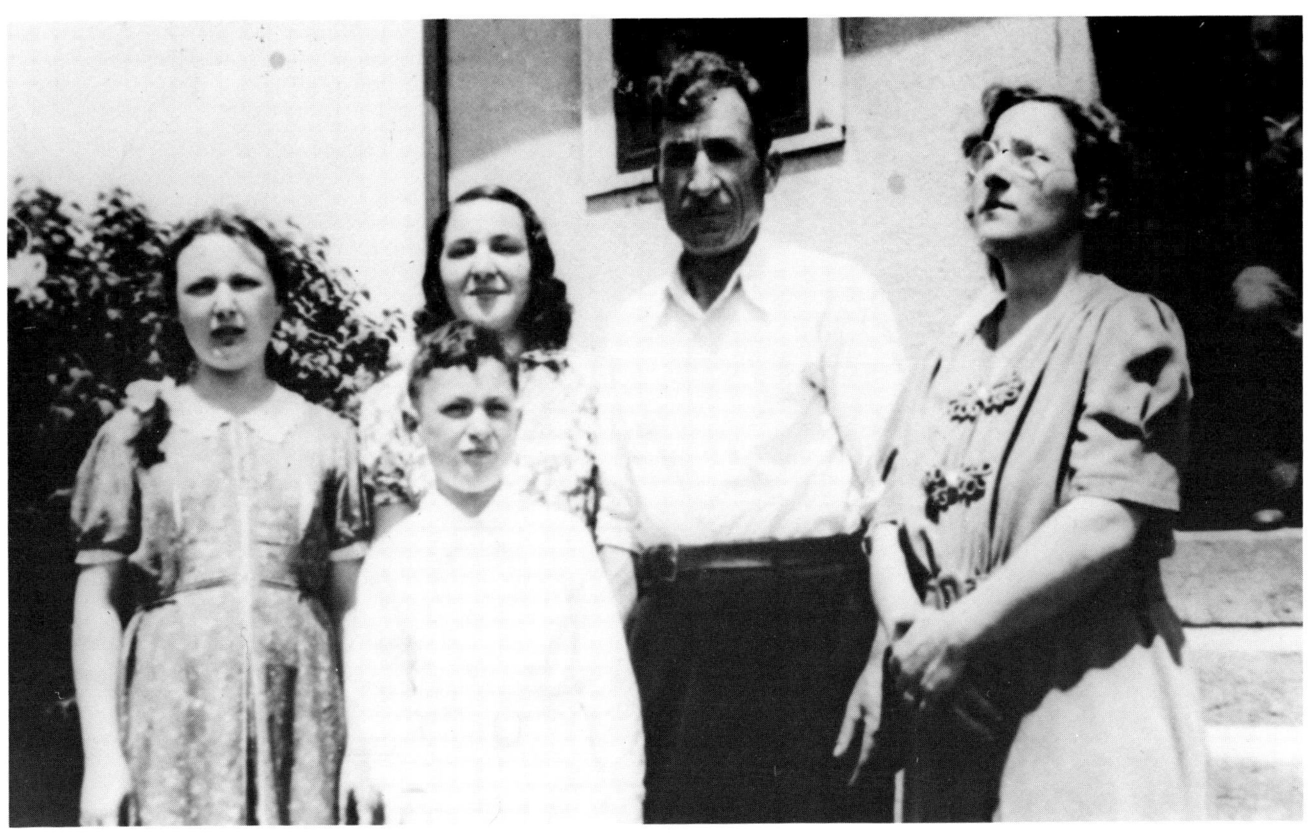

Dominick and Felice (Imparato) Volpecello with their children: Vansatta, John and Angie.

Mrs. Anna Cattano talks to her daughter on her wedding day. **1947.**

Sylvester and Minnie Pisciotto with their wedding party. **1924.**

Pellegrino and Angelina Esposito (left) celebrate at home with friends.

Michael and Santa Lucia with their children.

The Morristown Band. **At the railroad station, 1925.**

Dinner given by Mayor John Todd (head of table) for Morristown Band and friends. **1915.**

Flagler Street's band tunes up: (standing) Jimmy Inglese, Frank Ruocco, Vincent DiFalco, Louis DiFalco; (seated) Ralph Inglese.

Rio Clemente practicing piano, before his future studies at the Juilliard School of Music in New York City.

Costanzo children at Christmastime. **1930's.**

The Andreorio children. **c. 1929.**

Marguerite and Angelo Bitondo with their children.

Antoinette Galdi (center) with her extended family. **1950's.**

The Andaloros and Antonaccios with friends at the World's Fair. **New York City, 1939.**

Carmella and Joseph Chiappa (head of table) with their children and grandchildren.

The Stirone and Lucia families eating dinner together.

Mr. and Mrs. Carmen Mascuillo with their children.

Mr. and Mrs. Carmen Mascuillo with their grandchildren.

Ralph and Tomasina Vigilante with their wedding party. **1921.**

Jeanette Farina and Joseph Esposito on their wedding day.

Nancy and John Simone with their children: Fanny, Pat and Angie.
1927.

Pat and Pauline (Galdi) Rocco with their children.

Angela and Rocco Calderado. **c. 1910.**

Mary and Lawrence Cassamasso at his gas station on Water Street. **c. 1930.**

Theresa and Anthony Soranno on their 50th wedding anniversary.

"They were powerful men and women. They had love in their eyes."

Erminia Costanzo

Daniel Simonutti with his grandson. **1937.**

Mrs. (Louis) Anna Frances Donnamaria. **c. 1925.**

Anna and Vincenzo Galdieri. **c. 1907.**

Jenny Meola and Louis Galdieri with their wedding party.

The Monday Night Social Club: Members of the Mosso, Galdieri, Juliano, Vigilante and Pellegrini families. **1941.**

Dominick La Canfora, Anthony Pirone and Louis Goduto.

Filippo Goduto, Angelo Pennucci and Thomas Gianquinto. **c. 1915.**

John Stirone, Joe Lucia and Pat Leccese. **1936.**

Zia Lucia Mainiero's grandchildren at The Neighborhood House: Joseph Mainiero (in uniform), Carmella, Philip and Betty Nodoro. **1940's.**

VII. Morristown Moves Downtown: The Community Reaches Out

"I think everyone who was born and raised on Flagler Street was also raised in The Neighborhood House; that was home."

Mrs. Nicolene DiPrimo

"They taught us about religion there—I didn't know the difference between Catholic and Protestant. My mother didn't complain if I walked that far up the hill. She knew where we were going when we said 'Avanti scola' ('I'm going to school')."

Mrs. Minnie Pisciotto

"The hardest part of my job is to clear children out at five o'clock when it's time to go home."

Mrs. Marie Pierson
Director of Neighborhood House
(1912-1937)

"The only time I could go out at night as a boy was when I went to The Neighborhood House. My Dad knew where I was."

Tommy Rago

Montescaglioso Club outing. **1955.**

With its gymnasium and book-filled library, The Neighborhood House provided a place for children who had little room to play at home.

Work was the focus of activity in an immigrant family. Life grew desperate if a man did not earn money. Italians recognized this in 1895 when they formed the Society de Mutuo Socarso, whose members paid weekly dues. If a member became ill, the Society paid him $5 a week to support his family. In the event of death, all members contributed $1 each to the bereaved survivors.

Parents preoccupied with survival had little time to worry that their children had no place to play, either on the streets or in flats crowded with big families and boarders. In 1899 some of Morristown's community leaders began to realize how hard the immigrants had to work to support their children. They were not the millionaires who had moved to Morristown in recent years, but people whose families had lived in the town for generations.

These community leaders raised money to construct a two-story, wooden building at the top of Flagler Street. The Neighborhood House was designed to meet many needs and purposes: There was a gymnasium, a library, an infirmary, a hall and several classrooms. Concerned community leaders and members of the Morristown Junior League, an organization of women interested in helping the community, helped staff the center.

At first the Italians forbid their children to step inside the building. They were suspicious of these Protestant "missionaries" from outside Flagler Street. They were afraid these strangers would try to convert their children.

Eventually, though, the daily schedule of activities proved to be an irresistible magnet for the children of Flagler Street. Through them, the first sustained and helpful contact between the Italian community and Morristown's citizens was established.

Many of ***Mrs. DiPrimo***'s childhood memories are associated with The Neighborhood House.

"I think everyone who was born and raised on Flagler Street was also raised in The Neighborhood House; that was home. I took cooking classes there, sewing classes, piano lessons, all of that. And our showers, too. We had no bathroom where we lived.

"On Saturday mornings I used to stand up by The Neighborhood House and wait for all the girls to arrive," added ***Mrs. Gertrude (Mainiero) Nodoro.*** "Then we all went inside together and took our showers." Friday night at The Neighborhood House was reserved for the boys.

"We used to have all our parties there," said ***Mrs. Minnie Pisciotto.*** "They would teach us how to sing, play games, taught us how to read, about Catechism. They taught us about religion—I didn't know the difference between Catholic and Protestant.

"My mother didn't complain if I walked that far up the hill. She knew where we were going when we said, 'Avanti scola' ('I'm going to school')."

Youngsters playing at side entrance of The Neighborhood House. **1930's.**

The center's "Well Baby" clinic which started in 1922 was popular with Flagler Street's mothers. Boys attended carpentry and manual training classes there, adults went "up the hill," to learn English and take classes in citizenship and wedding receptions were held there.

The resident directors were Aldus and Marie Pierson who, as teetotalers, would not allow any wine, liquor or beer on the premises for any occasion—including wedding receptions.

Louis Goduto, remembering those rules, laughed. "The wedding party would store the wine, beer and liquor in a nearby store—ours, because it was next door. After a couple of hours—when Mr. and Mrs. Pierson weren't around—the wedding party would come into our store and sneak the liquor into The Neighborhood House and have a good time."

Mrs. Pierson, who kept order with an unruffled calm, used to remark that the "hardest part of my job is to clear children out at five o'clock when it is time to go home." Oldtimers still remember Mr. Pierson's demanding drills when he taught lively boys how to parade march with precision.

Although classes ended at 5 o'clock, the center was open in the evenings for dances and basketball. ***Tommy Rago,*** whose father owned a shoe repair shop, said, "The only time I could go out at night as a boy was when I went there. My Dad knew where I was. On Mondays and Wednesdays I was playing basketball at The Neighborhood House. That was the place for us. On those nights I could stay out until 10 o'clock. Other nights I had to be home."

Jim Costanzo recalled their boys' club that met at The Neighborhood House each week. "We had a rule that if anyone cursed he would be fined 5¢. We had one member, Johnny, who paid a dollar. When I was president, Rosario Clemente was going to some school and learning big words. There was a discussion when he used the word 'indubitably.' I immediately fined him 5¢. We had never heard the word."

The Morristown YMCA, uptown on Washington Street, and Cauldwell Playground, at the foot of Flagler Street hill, also attracted athletic youngsters. "I played every sport they had," recalled ***John Giordano;*** "baseball, handball, tennis, softball, horseshoes, everything. 'Champ' Kelly, who assisted Mr. Fairlamb, the big boss, and 'Pee Wee' Antonaccio had things under control. We had a lot of good athletes down there."

One Friday night, Jim Costanzo related, "We went to the Y, kids from nine to 12 years old. Mr. Lawton was the director. We all got undressed to our shorts, ready to play basketball.

"Mr. Lawton looked at us and said, 'Where are your sneakers?' We looked at him. Never heard the word sneakers. 'Alright, take off your shoes and go play basketball.' We ran onto the court in our stocking feet. After that, we went to the upper track over the court and

The Neighborhood House, with Goduto's Butcher Shop next door. **1927.**

ran until we got tired. Then into the swimming pool, after that a shower. From there we got dressed and went to a room where we got cocoa and cookies for 5¢.

Another Morristown "institution" during the 1920's was Mayor John Todd, who is still remembered fondly.

"Mayor Todd would come down to Flagler Street in a horse and wagon," said ***Michael Romano,*** "and later in a car with Ben Mucci driving. The Mayor was paralyzed in both legs and always stayed in the car.

"I liked the way he would stop on Sunday and talk to all the old Italian folks gathered at the top of the street. He shook hands with them and that made everybody happy.

"Even though the Italians spoke little English, the Mayor had a way of communicating. He gestured, 'How are you and how's the family?' The people responded. There was warmth there; the respect he had for us and we had for him."

These were a few of the signs that the isolation of the Italian community was slowly lessening. The men and women who staffed The Neighborhood House and Cauldwell Playground had been the first to penetrate that barrier with their sincere and helpful concern.

The Italian's labor had taken him up and out of "The Hollow," and he was beginning to make his mark on Morristown. The annual report issued by The Neighborhood House in 1913 noted that "Morristown's finest buildings have been constructed by Italian workmen."

Slowly, strangers were becoming neighbors.

Summer kindergarten class at The Neighborhood House. **1924.** *(Courtesy of the Curtiss Collection.)*

Treading the boards: Neighborhood House girls get ready for the stage. **1924.** *(Courtesy of the Curtiss Collection.)*

Marie and Aldus Pierson (near top of steps), co-directors of The Neighborhood House, with their teaching staff: Effie Kennedy, Lenore Tonkin, Janet Fraser and Jerry Scinto. **c. 1915.**

Marie Pierson at her 80th birthday party, with her daughter, (Mrs.) Helen Hettinger, and son, Albert. At the Morristown Women's Club. **1947.**

Neighborhood House girls exercising with Olive Gruber. **At Cauldwell Playground, 1925.**

Florin ("Pee Wee") Antonaccio, groundskeeper for Cauldwell Playground.

Mrs. Thomas Cauldwell, whose husband donated the land for Cauldwell Playground.

Flagler Street mothers and children at the opening of the "Well Baby" clinic sponsored by The Neighborhood House. **1922.** *(Courtesy of The Curtiss Collection.)*

Cauldwell Playground Girls' Baseball Team. **c. 1920.**

Boys in the library of The Neighborhood House: (back) Ernest Pignona, Pat Zarra, Gerry Gervasio; (front) unidentified and Larry Mainiero. **1910.**

Champs! The District Four Senior Baseball Team of Cauldwell Playground: (back row) Champ Kelly, assistant director of Cauldwell Playground, (unidentified), Pat Leccese, John Terreri, Mr. Fairlamb, Cauldwell Playground director; (front row) Angelo ("Tuts") Rich, Joe Giordano, Andrew Nodoro, R. Sar Mischiara, Tony Bontempo and Sam Verrilli.

Children on a slide outside The Neighborhood House. **1925.**

(Mrs.) Minnie Cherello with members of the "Tuscan Boys Club" at The Neighborhood House. **c. 1935.**

Together. **At The Neighborhood House, c. 1927.**

In the library at The Neighborhood House. **1924.** *(Courtesy of the Curtiss Collection.)*

Exercising in the new gymnasium-track of the Morristown YMCA. **1925.**

Neighborhood House basketball team. **1920.**

At the Y. **1928.**

Neighborhood House kids with their coaches (back row): Bucky Jones, Ralph Maietta and Bud Kronenberg. **c. 1935.**

Cauldwell Playground Junior Championship Baseball Team with their coaches (back row) Champ Kelly, Pat Vigilante and Mr. Fairlamb; (center) Joe Nocero, (unidentified), Frank Gerardi, Rocky Vigilante, Jimmy DeNunzio, John DeFilippis; (seated) Jimmy Vigilante and Russell Terreri. **1920.**

Neighborhood House Basketball Team, with Coach Dan Cacchio (top row, center). **1942.**

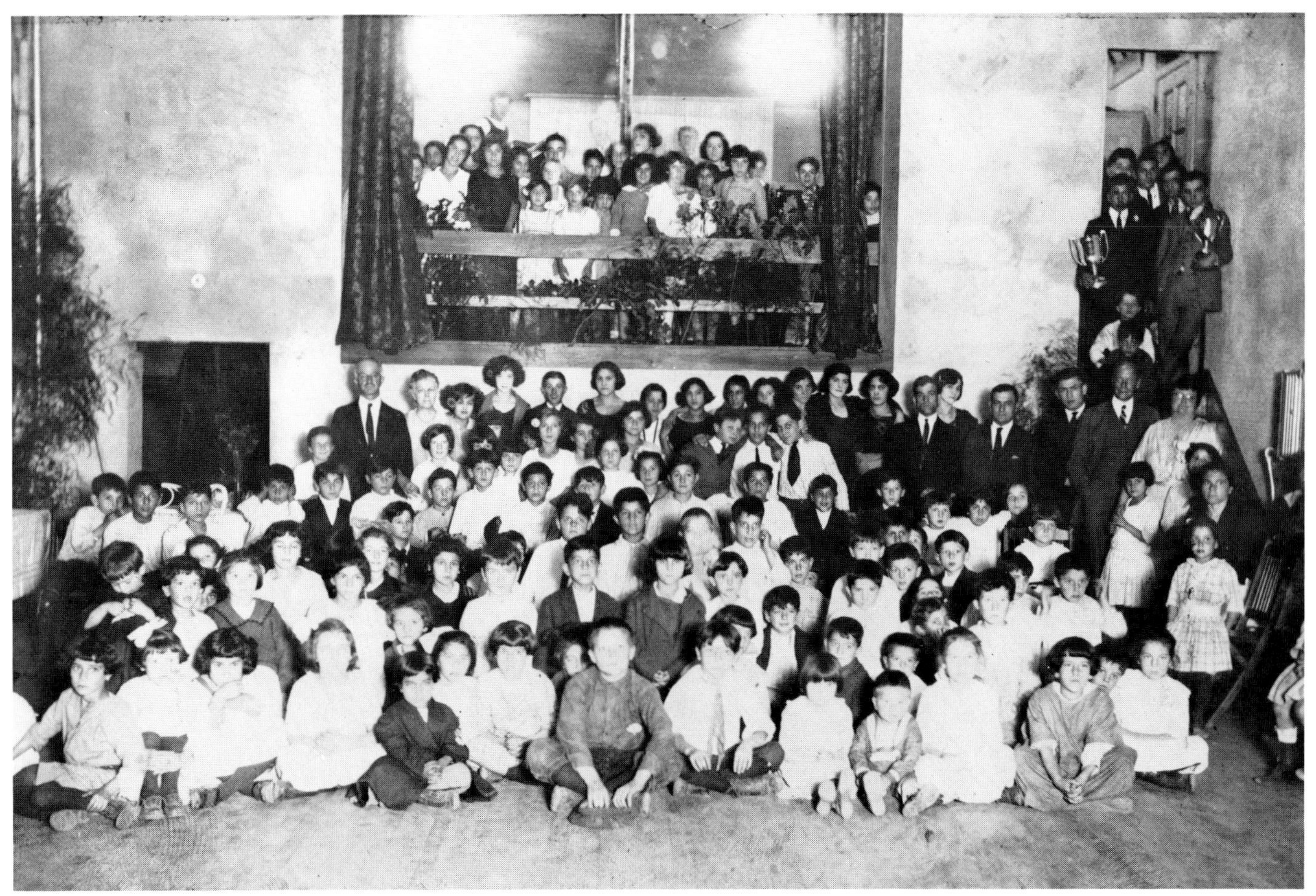

Dedication of the new gymnasium at The Neighborhood House. **1922.**

Girls attending a Neighborhood House dance, with (Mrs.) Minnie Cherello (far left) and (Mrs.) Adelaide Scerbo (far right) as chaperones. **1940's.**

"The Queen of Cauldwell Playground," Rose DeNunzio, (center), with her attendants. **1911.**

Girl Scouts at The Neighborhood House. **c. 1937.**

At Cauldwell Playground: Mrs. Liz Biele with daughter Liz next to (back row) cousins Rose Russo and Rose Russo, John Gervasio, Genevieve Trullo, Tony Terreri, Lottie DeFilippis, Gus Trullo, and Lucy Costanzo. (Front row): John Elia, Anna Mastrafano, Annette Sparano, Mike Soranno and Jean Simmarano.

On the fence: (l-r) Jean Simmarano, Lucy Costanzo, Annette Sparano, Rose Russo and Helen Bozzi. **1929.**

Neighborhood House kids: all grown up. **1930.**

"Bucky Jones," Robert Caravaggio's professional ring name. **1930.**

The ability to meet challenges head on was a skill that met with success in sports . . . Men like "Bucky Jones" (Robert Caravaggio) and Dan Cacchio were role models for young Italian boys.

Manager Bucky Jones with Bunky Wall, New Jersey Middleweight Champ. **1940.**

Carmine Vigilante (center) with sons Joseph, Louis, Rocco (kneeling), James and Arthur, who won the Morris County Basketball Championship. **1932.**

Playing bocci *outside The Neighborhood House.* **1948.**

Mary and Rocco Cifrese with their sons (clockwise): Vito, Liborio, Leonard and Paul. **c. 1925.**

VIII. The Immigrants Move Uptown: Taking Root

"When I was 19, I got a job as manager of the Mutual Grocery Store in Cedar Knolls. One day I ran a special: A greased pig to anyone who could catch it. A big gang of kids showed up to try to catch the prize.

"Who do you think caught it? Johnny Gervasio, Tony Pennucci, Joseph Catizone and other kids from Flagler Street. We all had a party with the roast pig. It was at the celebration in back of Clemente's Candy Store on Water Street; Al Gervasio got Judge Howard Bassett to speak to us.

"The date was October 14, 1932, and it was at the party that we got the idea we should form a club, a civic club, not a political club. We didn't want to be used by politicians. We wanted to take part in the civic life of Morristown.

"So on that day we formed the Young Men's Italian Club, later changed to the Morristown Columbian Club."

Tony Galdi

Verrilli's delivery truck on Race Street. **1922.**

By the early 1920's, business in "The Hollow" was brisk. Stores served the growing number of immigrants arriving each month from Italy, along with well-to-do Morristown residents.

Italian businessmen also worked for uptown residents. The Bontempo-D'Annunzio Construction Company and the Landi Excavating Company dug foundations and raised new buildings; the Tartaglia Tailor Shop specialized in custom-made suits for the wealthy; and Giordano's Grocery served the rich people who telephoned in their orders for home delivery.

Immigrant businessmen believed in the Italian proverb: "Deal with people better than you are, and you will get ahead."

Joseph and Robert Sagarese, for example, expanded their father's plumbing business by installing heating systems. "We did a lot of work in those big houses on Millionaire's Row on Madison Avenue—the Cranes, the Watts, Cutlers, Mellons and Colgates. We had a good bunch of customers, nice people and a lot of work," said ***Joseph Sagarese.***

Eney Grupelli and Leonardo Verrilli were two community leaders whose business influence extended beyond Flagler Street. Mr. Grupelli, an engineering teacher from Milan, built homes and buildings in Morris and in nearby Somerset County. Mr. Verrilli, who became a baker by chance, made acquaintances throughout Morris County on his daily deliveries.

The Grupelli Contracting Company contracted masonry, carpentry, landscaping and engineering work through offices on Flagler Street and uptown at 4 Washington Street.

"Mr. Grupelli drove me to work in his Model T," recalled ***Anthony Cherello.*** "He would take seven or eight men, all squeezed into his car, and drive us from Flagler Street out to Mendham and Gladstone where we worked on his contracting jobs.

"The oldtimers looked up to him for leadership and help. He wrote letters for the men when they were able to send for their wives to come from Italy."

After losing his wife and three children in Italy, Mr. Verrilli visited a friend in Morristown and decided to stay because the countryside reminded him of Italy.

At first he worked on the railroad, but later went into business for himself when a friend commented, "This town needs a good Italian bakery. More *paesani* are coming here each day." He persuaded Max Mintz, who was a cattle dealer and owned a house next door to him on Race Street, to lend him land and money to build a bakery. Knowing nothing about making bread and pastries, he imported bakers from New York City.

The bakery was an immediate success, although most of his customers lived outside "The Hollow." Most of the Italian women made their own bread.

Leonardo's daughter from his first marriage, now Mrs. ***Mary Petrozzo,*** recalled those early years.

"My father and mother baked the bread at night and delivered it the next morning. If he got home at two or

Verrilli's Bakery. **1930s.**

three in the afternoon, he made another trip in the horse and wagon. In any kind of weather. In winter the horses had screws under their shoes so they wouldn't slip."

It wasn't necessary to read or write to succeed. ***Arthur Fiori's*** father, for example, opened a fruit stall, expanded into the wholesale meat business and later invested in real estate. He left 87 parcels of real estate when he died. "He never had one day of school," his son said. "The only time he stepped inside a school was the day he came to see me graduate from eighth grade."

The late ***Dominick Costanzo***, an early businessman who later invested in real estate, insisted his sons follow one rule in doing business. "Your credit is the most important thing in business. If you cannot meet a note on a certain day, tell the bank and promise payment on a day when you can pay. Keep your credit good." Once obtained after much effort, credit—like honor—was a sacred obligation.

"Those Italian men of the 1920's, you'll never see men like them again," said ***Frank DiPrimo.***

"In one generation they accomplished more than any other and gave their children examples," stressed ***Anthony Tartaglia.***

Mary Petrozzo added, "Everybody worked hard. There were no lazy people; if they were lazy, they were outcasts. 'You don't want to work? Too bad. You get nothing.' They would be out."

"It's hard to figure how you get ambition," reflected ***Erminia Costanzo,*** "You want to better yourself and to better yourself, you've got to do it on your own. That's the way. Some people couldn't make it back then. Some went back to Italy. It was very hard.

"But then some life and spirit comes, and you try it different ways and it comes a little better. You know how to do it then, and you take a chance another time. You let loose and then you hold back."

From the beginning, social organizations were vital to life on Flagler Street. Mutual aid societies were founded out of necessity to aid the unemployed laborer, and social clubs, like the Montescaglioso Society and the Sons of Italy, were founded for enjoyment. Civic clubs, like the Columbian Club, gave young Italian men the opportunity to participate in the town's civic life.

As a kid of five in 1925," recalled ***Ralph Cangelosi,*** "I went with my parents on the Sons of Italy excursion to Long Branch in the summer. Whenever we left Morristown we brought our lunches—chickens, food and wine. Sometimes the bus broke down two or three miles on the way," he said with a chuckle.

These organizations were not only important to survival, but to self-image as well. An early incident known as "The Italian Revolt" in 1914 made this unquestionably clear.

A church survey of several neighborhoods in Morristown, including the Italian community, resulted in a photographic exhibit uptown which attracted 2,000 visitors. Women from Flagler Street were pictured carrying bundles on their heads, and children in shabby clothes

Frank Giordano (center) in his grocery store with (l-r): Mr. Driscoll, Mr. Shaw and sons Frank and Joseph.

were seen playing in cluttered backyards.

A crowd of 300 Italian men armed with clubs marched uptown to confront school officials. They were angry because their wives and children had been insulted. While they were talking, 20 others stormed into the exhibit and ripped up the offensive photographs.

As Italian families struggled to survive they found themselves facing many obstacles of discrimination.

Italian-born children, uncertain of their English, hesitated to enter into class discussions or raise their hands to answer a teacher's questions.

Rocco Nodoro recalled, "In school (about 1915), when I was in the second or third grade, the teacher made us stand and salute the flag and then asked whoever was not born in America to raise his hand. I raised my hand and then it began with the other kids: 'Guinea, Wop,' like that. We were always humiliated, like there was something wrong with us.

"Later on, in the fifth grade, the teacher asked us to write a composition about any trip we had taken. American kids wrote about a trip to New York or to the shore or to a museum. When it came our time to read our composition—well, what could we write about? Going to the dump to dig for coal?"

For years it was easier for a man to open a business than move his family out of "The Hollow." Some people in uptown neighborhoods flatly—and at the time legally—refused to sell their homes to Italian families. When the Vigilantes sought to buy a home in the Collinsville section, a friendly real estate man bought the house in his name for the Vigilantes.

Hard times also tested the immigrants' will to survive. During World War I, Italian families who had left Italy only a few years before wept as they sent their husbands and sons off to fight against relatives.

Later on, Prohibition brought illegal stills to the area at a time when certain Italian operators ran rackets in nearby big cities; as a result, all Italians suffered from the gangster stereotype.

The Great Depression found many Italians—the newest minority group—"the last hired and first fired," out of work and desperately poor. ***Sam D'Angelo*** recalled that "the Italians were too proud to go on relief. During the Depression, I would go up to Spring Street where the American Legion building was and pick up food, flour, everything, and carry it back in a wagon to Flagler Street."

As survival became less of an everyday crisis later in the 30's, some parents insisted their sons and daughters finish high school. Some began encouraging their sons to think about going to college. Neighbors signed notes for parents seeking educational loans for their children, and money was saved for years.

The story of E. Marco Stirone, later Mayor of Morristown (1965-1967), illustrates that where there is a will, there is a way.

Danny Mainiero owned the Washington Boot Black Parlor where Marco worked after school. He told the boy

Retirement dinner for Douglas Consalvo from the New Jersey Public Service and Electric Gas Company. **Summit, New Jersey, 1951.**

that if he really wanted to go to college—as he said he did—he would help him by saving the boy's wages in a "shoebox." Four year later, when Marco was graduated from Morristown High School, there was $900 in "The Shoebox Fund," which Mr. Mainiero had deposited every week at the National Iron Bank uptown. With that and money earned from other jobs, Marco became one of Flagler Street's first law school graduates.

Italians began joining fraternal groups like the Eagles. "In 1932 I became very active in that organization," said ***John Chiappa.*** "A lot of Italians, Irish and other nationalities belonged to the Eagles. I went all through the chairs and became president in 1934. In 1952 I was elected State President."

As Italian immigrants moved up—and away—from Flagler Street to buy or build homes uptown or in the growing towns surrounding Morristown, other nationalities moved in.

The flats with their balconies and porches are long gone, replaced by brick apartments, but The Neighborhood House and Cauldwell Playground continue to help Flagler Street's youngsters.

Uptown, sophisticated office buildings rising to 10 stories overlook the little park, known as The Green, in the center of town.

Morristown has changed with the times, but one thing has always stayed the same: It remains a place of opportunity. In the 1770's, it was the military headquarters of the Continental Army; in the 1890's, the favored retreat of the new millionaire industrialists; and in the 1980's Morristown is a prestigious address for major corporations.

Although many descendants of the early Italians have moved out of the area, those who remain have since become established.

The Italian community no longer is found on Flagler Street. It lives in the hearts of those who can find inspiration in the immigrant heritage of struggle and success.

"The Washington Bootblack Parlor." **1920.**

The "Washington Bootblack Parlor" changed names when its owner, Danny Mainiero, felt he had become "financially secure and socially acceptable as an Italian."

"D. Mainiero Shoes/Bootblack Parlor." **1922.**

(Mrs.) Rosina Stirone with her son, Marco, then mayor of Morristown, and daughters Genevieve, Adele, Minnie, Jennie and Louise at the Columbian Club. **c. 1965.**

Phyllis Azzara with her parents, Charles and Antonia. **1955.**

Eney and Nina Grupelli with their son, Logan. **c. 1905.**

THE JERSEYMAN, MORRISTOWN N. J.,

FRIDAY, OCTOBER 16 1914

ENEY GRUPELLI

GENERAL CONTRACTOR

Concrete and Re-inforced Concrete Work

Landscape and Engineering Work.

Teams, Farming Tools

Italian Laborers

TELEPHONE 469

No. 1 FLAGLER ST.

MORRISTOWN N. J

Eney Grupelli, a prominent contractor, advertises in 1914.

Logan Grupelli with his wife, Dorothy. **1950's.**

Marietta and Lucio Tartaglia with their son, Anthony, and daughter, Beatrice. **1940's.**

Adam and Lucio Tartaglia (foreground) in their tailor shop. **1930's.**

Leonardo Verrilli (l) with his twin brother, Carmine, visiting from Bridgeport, Conn. **c. 1910.**

The immigrant proverb advised, "Do business with people better than you and you will get ahead."

Antonia Verrilli, Leonardo's wife and business partner.

Once obtained after much effort, credit—like honor—was a sacred obligation.

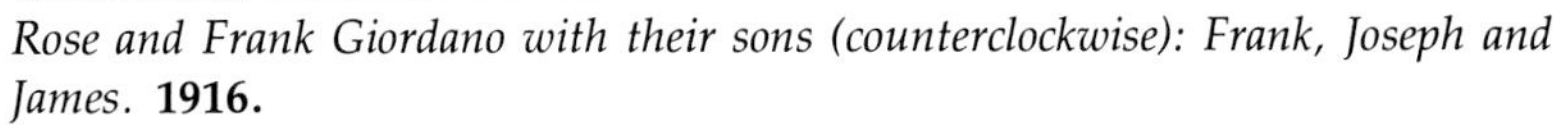

Rose and Frank Giordano with their sons (counterclockwise): Frank, Joseph and James. **1916.**

Frank Giordano in front of his first store at 120 Speedwell Avenue.

Louis Tremallo, Flagler Street's first Italian magistrate.

Retiring Morristown magistrate, R. Sar Mischiara, (standing) turns over his office to his successor, Harold Gurevitz (l), as New Jersey Superior Court Judge Edward F. Broderick (r) officiates. **1965.**

Nicholas Marinaro in front of The Flatiron Building on Speedwell and Sussex Avenues, which he built in 1920.

Donald Cresitello, former Mayor of Morristown. **1981.**

Nancy Racamato and Frank Landi with their parents, Michael and Anne Racamato, and Rose and Thomas Landi, on their wedding day. **1947.**

The Landi brothers: Frank, Carmen, Anthony and John with nephew Thomas (center).

Mrs. Carmen (Michelene) Pagano's parents, Paul and Maria Chiodo, with their daughter, Lentine. **c. 1912.**

Pellegrino and Bridget (Rago) Pagano with their children: Anthony, Vincent, Olympia, Ann, Margaret, (Dr.) Lewis and Carmine.

A gathering of the Azzara and Butera families.

Luigi and Maria Giovanna Meola. **c. 1940's.**

Anthony and Addolorata Gerardi. **1930's.**

Joseph and Lillian Cattano with their daughters, Mary and Rose.

Tony Cattano (former mayor of Morristown), with his mother, Lillian and: (seated) his sister, Rose Cattano, Mrs. (Vincent) Anna Cattano and daughter, his wife, Mrs. Rose Cattano and Josephine Cattano. **1947.**

Family: (standing) Florence Gervasio, Mrs. (John) Katie Gervasio, Letizia and Emilio Gervasio (current mayor of Morristown), John Gervasio; Gerald Gervasio, Maria DeFilippis, Antonio Gervasio, Mrs. (Gerald) Bertha Gervasio and son, Jimmy.

Dominick and Grace (Pennucci) Terreri with their family: (back row) Norman, Robert Clements, Thomas and Dominick Jr.; (front row) Mrs. Adelia (Terreri) Clements, Mr. and Mrs. Angelo (Nancy) Terreri.

Joseph and Angelica Terreri with their children, Mary, Clara and Dominick. **1910.**

Frances (Simone) Rocco on her graduation from nursing school. **1947.**

"Nobody had much, and our mothers and fathers couldn't speak English, but their children turned out pretty well. They learned trades and went to school and did well for themselves. And now their children are doing even better, going to college and getting into business and professional fields."

Tony Elia

Raffaella and Sabino Moschella with their daughter, Ann, (standing) and son, Joseph. **1924.**

Epilogue: Looking Ahead

"I had in mind a subjective history—what was in their hearts and minds; their innermost thoughts, secrets, ambitions, desires. To tell the story from inside the person—that is what we wanted to penetrate . . ."

James V. Costanzo, Sr.
July, 1982

End of an era: The Grupelli Flats are demolished to make way for Morristown's Urban Renewal Project. **1950's.**

There was a knock at the door.

Jim Costanzo looked up. "Who is it?" he asked. He had been working late in his office at the Morris County courthouse in Morristown.

A young woman poked her head inside the door. She motioned with mop and pail.

"It made me sad that this nice young woman's first job in America was so menial. I was embarrassed for her. After she was finished, I stopped working and asked her where she was from. 'Colombia, South America,' was all she could say in English. I wanted to know more, but she couldn't understand. I made a motion with my hands, a 'thumbs up' sign; I figured it was the universal good luck symbol.

"I wanted her to know that I believed in her, that if she worked hard and saved her money, she could make it in this country. If she kept doing her best, I said in sign language, the future would give her better jobs.

"Why could I believe that? Because I was the son of immigrants myself and yet I was working on the other side of that desk as surrogate.

"I remembered that my parents and grandparents, and all the other Italian immigrants I had known, had had a tough time too back in the early 1900's.

"It was hard for them, and it would be hard for this new immigrant. Times are tough today, but this country is still a place of opportunity."

Hard work overcomes many obstacles, as ***Tony Tartaglia*** likes to tell me. "You know," he has often said, "when our parents came to America, they were illiterate, but they were not unintelligent just because they couldn't read or write English. The had the genes; America gave them the opportunity.

"We saw them work hard, and we learned that if we wanted to get ahead, we had to work too. My father worked from seven in the morning until 10 at night in his tailor shop. He raised us kids, bought a house and helped us get an education. When we went to school, we knew we had to study and make good. We got that drive from our parents."

Back then, ***Tony Elia*** pointed out, "Nobody had much, and our mothers and fathers couldn't speak English. But their children turned out pretty well. They learned trades and went to school and did well for themselves. And now their children are doing even better, going to college and getting into business and professional fields.

"The opportunities are there if you are willing to work. That's one trait the immigrants had: They worked day and night to lift themselves up. We should always remember where we came from and be proud of our traditions and heritage."

"I thought about that young woman as we worked on the book," said Jim Costanzo. "Wherever she is, I'd like her and others like her to know this: Nobody owns the American Dream. It belongs to anyone willing to humble himself and work hard."

Making memories: family party at the home of Patsy DeRuggiero.

Backyard get-together: The Vincent DiFalco and Nicholas Ruocco families.

Leopold Mischiara with his wife and children.

"We saw our parents work hard, and we learned that if we wanted to get ahead, we had to work too . . . We got that drive from our parents."

Tony Tartaglia

Emilio and Amelia Caravaggio with their children (l-r): Dominick, Fanny and Robert.

Cesaria and Michael Bozzi (center) with their children. **1940's.**

Angelo and Josephine Crisante. **c. 1915.**

Margaret and Salvatore Loia on their 50th wedding anniversary. **1978.**

Philip and Elizabeth Oropallo with Helen and Dominick Pisciotto.

Anniversary dinner for Paul and Mary Danna (seated, center), with (l-r) Mr. and Mrs. Michael Galdi, Mary and Frank Petrozzo and Minerva and Matthew Appio attending.

Mary and Joseph Parmigiani (seated, left) with their sons John, Louis, Joseph and Anthony and daughter, Marie. **1930's.**

The Camisas, grandchildren of Morristown's first-known Italian immigrants: Paul, Jack, Pauline, Catherine and Marie.

Rose and Frank Cecala.

Rose DeVito and Michael Levato with their wedding party. **1928.**

Gertrude Mainiero and Andrew Nodoro with their wedding party. **1929.**

Anna DiCarlucci and James Giordano with their wedding party. **October 9, 1933.**

Fannie Bozzi and John Marinaccio with their wedding party.

Antonio and Maria Santangelo with their son, Ernest, on his wedding day. **1950.**

Mr. and Mrs. Andrew (Gertrude Mainiero) Nodoro. **October 10, 1929.**

Rose and Alfonso Giordano on their wedding day with Rose Levato, maid of honor, and Antonio Costanzo, best man. **1920.**

Michael Pennucci (seated) with his grandchildren on the wedding day of his granddaughter, Lucille DiPrimo, to Robert Mooney. (Great-granddaughter Diane DiPrimo is sitting on his lap.) **1957.**

". . . The children of Italian immigrants no longer feel Italian: They are American . . . In shedding a sense of apartness from American life, they have also relinquished their once-powerful emotional association with a remote Italian world they knew secondhand, from family recollections and legends. A void has been created . . .

Louis and Florence Todero with their wedding party.
April 21, 1928.

Vito and Maria Soranno with their children: Pat, Angelina, Mike, Joseph and Dominick.

Nicholas and Concetta Cazzetto with their children and grandchildren.

Rosemarie DiNola (Granchelli) on her wedding day with her grandparents, Antoinette and Samuel Dante. **c. 1961.**

". . . and they are now beginning to reevaluate their ethnic past—which is Italian American rather than Italian—because it is an inescapable part of what they think about themselves, and what they tell their children."

Erik Amfitheatrof

Index of Photographs

T

U

V

W

Z